PRAISE FOR *INNER FIRE*

This is the book I wish I had earlier in my corporate career. Based on Lisa Wolfe's extensive experience and sage insights, *Inner Fire* provides practical guidance for professionals seeking to avoid burnout and thrive in the corporate world.

—Kathryn W. Guarini, PhD

Senior fellow, Yale University; director, Regeneron; former chief information officer, IBM

Inner Fire masterfully blends authenticity with practical wisdom, offering readers a road map to navigate the corporate landscape without losing sight of their inner essence. This compelling read provides valuable insights and tools for achieving harmony between personal fulfillment and professional success, making it essential for those striving to thrive in both realms. A must-read for anyone navigating corporate life who is interested in aligning their inner essence with external success.

—Katherine Aitken

CXO Initiatives, Content Experience

Good corporate warriors don't let their spirits be the collateral damage. As a former colleague who witnessed firsthand how Lisa managed to do that in corporate combat, I urge you not to miss out on this special book, where she divulges what it takes to not just be a better worker but also a better partner, a better parent, and a better human.

—Joe Leung
Product marketing director, OpenText Cybersecurity

In her book *Inner Fire*, Lisa Wolfe, a trailblazer and pioneer woman business leader with forty years' experience in the technology field, shares insightful wisdom and practical guidance gleaned from her corporate journey. Through her Spirit-Keeper method, she extends an invitation for readers to join the Spirit-Keeper Tribe. Offering practical strategies and inspiring narratives, this book serves as a road map to infuse purpose and passion into both professional and personal lives. It's not merely a book; it's a lifeline for those navigating the corporate world, ensuring they not only avoid burnout but also thrive as integral members of the Spirit-Keeper Tribe. This is essential reading for anyone seeking fulfillment and direction in their career and life.

—Lisa Rawls
Advisory partner, KPMG LLP

I've worked in a large government laboratory, large computer company, small technology innovation companies, and now have been teaching at a university for over thirty years (and have maintained active consulting). Some things that I deal with every day are:

- How do I keep myself from "retiring in place"?
- How can I mentor leaders through example?
- How can I support my colleagues to "next-level" achievements?

The key is *Inner Fire*.

Lisa has clearly articulated the process and mentality to prevent burnout and to maintain vitality in the workplace. Her "lessons learned" clearly shows a path to stay focused and engaged, even with what we might consider mundane and routine tasks that we all encounter in our work lives.

Geez, I'll reread *Inner Fire* to fire me up because sometimes we all could use some reignition.

—Ernie Kim, PhD, PE
Professor of electrical engineering, Shiley-Marcos School of Engineering, University of San Diego

In this insightful and compelling book, the author beautifully bridges the gap between the resilience of the human spirit and the intense demands of the corporate world. Drawing on firsthand experiences, this book offers a powerful exploration of how to maintain one's spirit amid life's challenges. It provides practical wisdom and moving stories, making it an essential guide for anyone looking to thrive professionally without sacrificing their inner essence. Truly a beacon of hope and strength for those seeking to find or retain their inner spirit and live a purpose-driven life.

—Patricia Grant
CIO, Tenable

Having worked in the corporate trenches with Lisa for over two years, I know her to be a true Spirit-Keeper, and I couldn't be happier that she has written this book! From both an analytical and a soulful approach, she helps us understand a workplace epidemic we all know exists, but few have been able to describe in such a meaningful but realistic way. Start reading this on your next business trip or one night after a long weekday, and I bet you will feel differently about work as a result.

—Evans Nicholson
Senior technical product and solutions marketing manager, IT Operations Management/CMDB/Telecommunications/Cloud Solutions, ServiceNow

Reading this book made me feel seen, empowered, and hopeful that I can take the actions necessary to be my own Spirit-Keeper! In a society where productivity is treated as the most important KPI, this book makes me wonder what incredible things we could be doing if sense of spirit was also just as valued. How much more engaged and purpose driven would we be? Thank you for sharing the unseen but everyday stories that many of us corporate warriors experience. Most of all, for reminding us we can flourish even more by embracing our humanity.

—Estella Gong
Senior solution consultant, ServiceNow

A dream job has the potential to be your life source, nurturing your intellectual curiosity and drive. It provides rewarding experiences that offer a sense of purpose and an escape, helping you to overcome the harsh realities and adversity found in everyday life.

I have had the good fortune to work with Lisa, a fellow traveler in the fast-paced, high-tech corporate world that is rapidly evolving through the advent of generative AI. In this highly complex and dynamic landscape, Lisa's intellect and compassionate guidance ensures that humanity remains at the core of how we advance this incredible technology.

With *Inner Fire,* Lisa extracts wisdom and provides highly relatable insights through observation and sharing of lived experiences from other "Spirit-Keepers"—people who nourish and protect their inner vitality and humanity by being like water, advocating for adaptability and resilience, particularly in this time of accelerated change in all aspects of life. This book offers not just insights but also transformative pathways to rekindle and nurture your spirit so you can be the best version of you.

—Sean Hughes
AI ecosystem director, ServiceNow

Inner Fire

Inner Fire

Lisa Wolfe

Advantage | Books

Published by Advantage Books, Charleston, South Carolina.
An imprint of Advantage Media.

Printed in the United States of America.

10 9 8 7 6 5 4 3 2 1

ISBN: 979-8-89188-084-9 (Paperback)
ISBN: 979-8-89188-197-6 (Hardcover)
ISBN: 979-8-89188-085-6 (eBook)

Library of Congress Control Number: 2024918647

Cover design by Matthew Morse.
Layout design by Ruthie Wood.

For Larry, Shelby, and Cody—the sparks to my flame.

CONTENTS

ACKNOWLEDGMENTS

I started this book decades ago and while it never left my soul, I found myself too busy with work and life to finish it. I am deeply indebted to my book partner and truly extraordinary editor, Diana Holquist, for helping me get this book written and out to the world. My hope for this book is that it will change the lives of corporate professionals for the better.

I am grateful to my developmental editor, Lauren Steffes, for raising thoughtful questions throughout the process, and encouraging me to dive deeper into certain topics to help readers get the greatest value from the lessons learned.

I'd like to extend my deepest gratitude to Kathryn Guarini, Ph.D. for her deep insights and guidance throughout the writing process. Kathryn led global Fortune 500 teams for many years, including as a former IBM CIO. There are hundreds of people I have worked and partnered with throughout the years—who I am so grateful for, and have been inspired by—and these people inspire others every day by being Spirit-Keepers. Special thanks to:

Steve Anderson, Manisha Arora, Katherine Aitken, Veronica Banda, Laura Beeler, Cathy Birkelbach, Amel Chehayeb, Isabelle Coste, Gemma Davies, Damien Davis, Jeremy Duncan, Dan Durller, Kimberly Eisendrath, Steve Emerson, Roni Fontaine, Dayna Fried,

Patricia Grant, Estella Gong, Shawnna Hoffman, Jon Huang, Sean Hughes, Mary Johnston-Turner, Maja Kaiser, Professor Ernie Kim–Ph.D., Britta Koch, Andy Krier, Laura LeBleu, Philip Lee, Joe Leung, Allison Lion, Jon Lion, DeVasha Lloyd, Amy Lokey, Gina Mastantuono, Evans Nicholson, Brad Parks, Lisa Rawls, Jonathan Riemer, Dina Saunders, Twisha Shah, Theo Simmons, Kelley Steven-Waiss, Emily Walker, Barbara Waugh—Ph.D., Toby Weiss, Matt Wickersham, and Jefferi Hamilton Wolfe.

And thank you to the loves of my life—Larry, Shelby, and Cody—all of whom have known this book for decades and have encouraged me to keep it alive.

INTRODUCTION

I started to write this book after a tragedy in which a loved one suffered a sudden accident. Week after week, month after month, my family sat with him in the hospital ward as he began his long journey back to independence. Spending that time with him was a profound privilege—a lesson in what the human soul is capable of surviving.

I watched as many patients on the ward faced the heart-wrenching reality not only of their new physical limitations but also of abandonment by some of their own families, who were overwhelmed by the emotional weight of their loved ones' new circumstances. I am deeply grateful for my family who had the opportunity to become a source of solace and companionship to some of these people, cultivating bonds of empathy amid overwhelming adversity.

In return, they gave me an unexpected and remarkable gift: a newfound perspective on my own world.

As I navigated back and forth between weekends at the hospital and weekdays consumed by the rigors of my corporate job, I realized that I had initially perceived these two environments as starkly divergent realms. Instead, the constant juxtaposition opened my eyes to a startling insight. Saturday and Sunday, I was surrounded by people struggling to survive unimaginable physical hardship, accompanied by profound emotional struggle. Monday through Friday, I was surrounded by ostensibly able-bodied individuals who, like my weekend friends, seemed to be fighting a challenging inner struggle to survive.

What was going on?

Many of my workmates had a visible loss of enthusiasm for daily work that was reflected in their vacant expressions and slumped shoulders. The relentless pressures and dynamic demands of the corporate world were damaging them, and I soon came to realize that my colleagues were suffering from a kind of spiritual paralysis that was the result of burnout. Burnout, as defined by the World Health Organization, is a syndrome "resulting from chronic workplace stress that has not been successfully managed" and characterized by "feelings of energy depletion … exhaustion; increased mental distance from one's job, or feelings of negativism or cynicism … and reduced professional efficacy."[1]

I call it a loss of inner spirit.

Burnout occurs for many different reasons, but working in the corporate world often involves confronting a barrage of demands that you cannot control and an hourly flood of texts, team chats, and Zoom meetings all happening simultaneously. There is no time for deep, meaningful work, and it is that deep, meaningful work that had once sustained you and brought you into the corporation in the first place. This constant chaos doesn't give you time to think, learn, or reflect, putting you in danger of losing your inner fire. A deep unhappiness seeps into the fabric of your life until doing anything feels overwhelming.

---

1 "Burn-out an 'Occupational Phenomenon,'" World Health Organization, accessed January 12, 2023, https://www.who.int/standards/classifications/frequently-asked-questions/burn-out-an-occupational-phenomenon.

As alarming as it was to recognize so much spiritual paralysis at my work, I saw a ray of hope: there were a few who managed to escape burnout. These bright lights not only managed to avoid spiritual paralysis, but their spirits were also *thriving*. They stood out among the blank looks, long sighs, and depressed postures around them. The health of their spirits sustained them in this environment that was so damaging to so many. I began to call these people Spirit-Keepers. It took me years to become a Spirit-Keeper myself. I learned much of my Spirit-Keeper knowledge and skills from the Spirit-Keepers in my network and from my own experiences navigating years of developing the skills to protect my spirit from corporate burnout.

How did we do it?

It became my central purpose to answer that question in a systematic way that would help others. My education was as a computer scientist, but my life's passion became to help people reconnect with their spirits. I set out to understand the Spirit-Keepers around me—how they were like me and how they were different. I needed to know what steps they took to preserve their passion for life in circumstances in which others couldn't. My goal was to create a comprehensive road map for resilience in the corporate world that others could embrace and apply to their own lives.

I already knew that I wouldn't find answers from the pundits who professed to be experts in corporate life. In my decades-long career in the corporate world, I have encountered my fair share of supposed experts on workplace happiness—from work-life coaches to consultants to academics from top universities. While their intentions were good, their workshops and advice ultimately left little to no impact on the real day-to-day quality of life of those around me. Often, their advice didn't lack data or credibility, but their "expertise" still missed a crucial ingredient: ***lived experience in the corporate world***. Having careers that were very different from those of us whom they preached to, they never seemed to understand the gravity of a corporation's impact on one's spirit or, more importantly, how to avoid its damage.

I, on the other hand, am a member of an exclusive club that includes four decades of technical and leadership experience in tech. I have had firsthand experience working with the major tech innovations of the last four decades. Since graduating from the University of California, San Diego (UCSD) in 1984 with a Computer Science degree, I have held roles in software engineering, technical solution consulting, product management, product marketing, and leadership. My work has focused on cutting-edge tech innovations, including cloud computing and artificial intelligence (AI), at major Fortune 500 corporations such as National Cash Register, Burroughs Corporation Advanced Systems Group, Hewlett-Packard, Seagate, and ServiceNow.

During this time I have seen firsthand how spirits die without warning, and I have fought hard and succeeded in keeping my own spirit intact. And what a ride this has been and still is. In terms of tech innovation alone, I've been part of a remarkable transformation, from my early days writing assembly language code to the exploration of generative AI.

> Rather, there were specific steps Spirit-Keepers took to create a life of meaning and purpose that kept their spirits intact in the corporate world.

Abandoning the experts, I looked to my own experience and the other Spirit-Keepers around me to try to understand what made us different. Through observation, research, formal interviews, and quite a few not-so-formal, late-night conversations, I came to understand that our unique mindset was not one we stumbled upon, nor was it an innate, unattainable gift of optimism or luck. Rather, there were specific steps Spirit-Keepers took to create a life of meaning and purpose that kept their spirits intact in the corporate world.

The Spirit-Keeper mindset can keep your vitality intact inside the corporation. By sharing what can be done to maintain your spirit within the context of current work conditions in the corporate world, I hope I will inspire you to become a leader who transforms the corporate culture to ease the path for yourself and your colleagues.

To hold on to a life of spirit within a corporation, I lay out the following three main principles:

- Sustaining your spirit requires a strong personal mission and values.
- Relationships, networks, and understanding and managing internal politics—not playing politics but understanding and being aware of internal dynamics so they don't run you over—are all key to keeping spirit strong.
- Change is the one constant in corporate life, and you must expect and prepare for it if you want to keep your spirit alive.

This book is filled with examples of people who followed these three basic principles, as well as those who didn't but eventually found their way. Every chapter is based on one of nine core lessons in spirit nourishment, advice, and inspiration and leaves room for you to reflect on your own experiences.

This book can also serve as a reference guide. If there is a specific topic or area you need support in or would like to learn more about, simply review that chapter or come back to it later when you need it most.

One question that came up again and again in my journey to understanding was, "Why stay? Why not leave the corporation to pursue a career elsewhere?"

Certainly, that is a valid path. However, I urge you to not abandon corporate life. Spirit-Keeping is not just about enduring; it's about thriving and leveraging the unique platforms for personal growth that corporations can provide. Corporations, despite their flaws, offer opportunities for personal growth, collaboration, and mentorship so that individuals can realize their full potential and make a lasting impact on the world around them. Growing up inside a corporation has enabled me to become a more complete human being. That said, I also recognize from my experience and research that some people, after careful reflection, realize that corporate life is not for them.

In addition to personal growth potential, corporations are key to the progress of humanity. While the corporate landscape may often seem daunting and unforgiving, I truly believe that navigating the complexities of corporate life while holding on to your spirit contributes to a better world for everyone. Only corporations and governments possess the financial and human resources necessary to enact significant positive change on a global scale—and we all know how inefficient, slow-moving, and unpredictable governments can be. I am not naively optimistic—I acknowledge that many corporations fall short of ethical standards. However, they rely on the dedication of ethical, purposeful, spirit-driven individuals to move humanity forward. Good people need to stay to make that happen.

I often think back to that hospital ward. A hospital is, for better or worse, a corporation. And it relies on other corporations—pharmaceuticals, medical equipment suppliers, and so on—to create life-changing innovations. The advances in treating patients like my loved one between when I was there and now are nothing short of miraculous.

As we continue to harness the true potential of technology and AI, we know that these and other innovations are having a profound impact on our world—both good and bad. As that future moves closer, we need the best people there to guide the ship. Corporations are, after all, just groups of people coming together to build something greater than they could as individuals.

We need good people to stay and to do the good work that needs to be done. For that to happen, these people need to find their inner spirit and hold on to it. A lot of what I advise in this book—like having clear boundaries and the importance of understanding and managing internal politics so you are aware and know what to avoid and what to bring in closer—is not what you're used to hearing in this age of being "vulnerable" and "authentic" at work. But that is why I am writing this book. I believe my insights, won over decades in the belly of the beast, can make a difference to individuals and, ultimately, to the larger world.

Corporations are, after all, just groups of people coming together to build something greater than they could as individuals.

To hold on to your spirit is not easy, but the payoff of being one of the people who are fully alive, fully empowered, and fully productive within a corporation is worth the fight. Spirit-Keepers create their own futures instead of letting the outside forces of the corporate environment shape them. And in this way, they shape the world.

If you are not already a Spirit-Keeper, this book will show the way forward.

Welcome to the tribe!

CHAPTER ONE

SPIRITS DIE WITHOUT WARNING

Recognizing burnout before it's too late

How we spend our days is, of course, how we spend our lives.

—ANNIE DILLARD, AMERICAN AUTHOR

Caroline W.,[2] a corporate change expert, stood on the stage, speaking to hundreds of executives about a breakthrough pay system she was managing. She was twenty-nine years old and a production manager of her company's hottest product. To everyone in the audience, she appeared the epitome of success, the example of how hard work, drive, and devotion to the corporation could pay off.

Suddenly, her knees locked up. She somehow finished her speech, hobbled off the stage, and began a journey into managing a life-changing diagnosis—an undifferentiated connective tissue disorder.

2 The information in this book has come from decades of interviews and experiences. Names and some identifying details, including the timing of various events, have been changed to preserve privacy and confidentiality.

This, she learned, was a form of rheumatoid arthritis that could ultimately lead to debilitating conditions and even death. Her doctors explained that it was an autoimmune disease, with symptoms that could be exacerbated by stress.

Was there, they asked, anything particularly stressful going on in her life?

Caroline was a corporate warrior, so of course there was. For two years Caroline had been working nonstop, literally seven days a week. Before that fateful day on the stage, she had been working every shift, with little to no sleep. This wasn't forced upon her. She was following her passion, creating a work system that would result in people bringing their hearts, minds, and expertise to their careers. She knew that her project could help bring profound changes to the work culture of her company, resulting in fundamental improvements for thousands of workers.

Yet, ironically, she didn't hear the whispers of her spirit dying at her job until she was hit with the crashing thunder of disease. Rheumatoid arthritis affects every joint. Caroline could not lift a coffee cup without being in severe pain. She was used to running in the fast lane for so long she did not even know where or how to begin to slow down and ask for help. She did not, at first, even realize she was dealing with more than a physical condition.

Caroline felt alone, but in fact, she had a lot of company facing what she would come to learn was corporate burnout. A recent study by Asana looked at over ten thousand workers across seven countries and found approximately 70 percent had experienced burnout in the last year. Among these, 84 percent of Gen Zs, 74 percent of millennials, and 47 percent of boomers reported experiencing burnout.[3] While not all of these cases were as extreme as Caroline's, they highlighted a widespread issue, with a significant number of workers across different generations feeling the impact of high-stress environments. These statistics show a concerning trend that extends beyond individual health to a collective workplace challenge.

Slowly, after a lot of introspection, research, and trial and error, Caroline figured out how to care for herself. When I met Caroline for the first time to interview her for this book six years after that day on the stage, she radiated the vitality of her thirty-six years. But when she spoke, she emanated the wisdom of someone who had lived much longer. She told me that she had "pushed the system beyond its limits" and hadn't even seen her crisis coming.

The first step to recognizing spirit loss is to understand what spirit means to you.

What Is Spirit?

The word "spirit" has many definitions, but for the purposes of this book, I define spirit as a person's energy: their vitality, passion, and natural inner fire.

Spirit for some is a religious idea, but it doesn't have to be. While traditionally associated with metaphysics, the concept of spirit can also be understood in secular terms, as a relationship to art, nature, humanity—and even to work.

In this latter sense, spirit is often described as a person's inner drive, passion, and resilience. That is the definition I focus on in this

---

3 "Anatomy of Work Special Report: The Unexplored Link between Imposter Syndrome and Burnout," Asana, accessed April 9, 2024, https://resources.asana.com/americas-anatomy-of-work-burnout-ebook.html.

book, but any definition of spirit that resonates with you is the one you should embrace. However you conceive of spirit, whether as a divine spark or deriving from another source, its presence is unmistakable when experienced.

As far as relating spirit to corporate life, I find psychologist Mihaly Csikszentmihalyi's writings on spirit helpful. He is known for his work on the concept of "flow," which describes being so engrossed in a project that we lose track of time and distractions. He links spirit to that state of flow, where "one's skills meet the challenges at hand."[4]

When we exist in the moment, without distraction, this is flow, and it is one key element that helps us preserve our spirits and do our best work. When you are working with people who have their spirits fully intact and cared for, you can feel their connection to the moment. They are giving 100 percent to the problem at hand. For example, when I am engaged in a new technology that I can see is changing the world, industries, and lives around me, my spirit is fully engaged and committed to seeing this new tech reach its full potential.

However you conceive of spirit, whether as a divine spark or deriving from another source, its presence is unmistakable when experienced.

I felt this kind of spirit engagement when the concept of "cloud" first entered the industry. At that time Hewlett-Packard had a technology called e-services that was cloud before cloud. Working on it gave me a sense of purpose and an energizing connection to my core—to my spirit. Csikszentmihalyi writes, "Intense concentration on the present … relieves us of the

4 Mihaly Csikszentmihalyi, *Flow: The Psychology of Optimal Experience* (New York: HarperCollins Modern Classics, 1991), 12.

usual fears that cause depression and anxiety in everyday life."[5] That is, it helps prevent burnout.

The Loss of Spirit

Tell me about your day. How does it unfold? Does your day blur together in the tiring buzz of messages, virtual and in-person meetings, team chats, and new projects put on your plate? Do you find yourself stretched thin, with no time to eat lunch or read a book? In extreme cases do you struggle to find time to pick up your child from school?

Have you told yourself you'd make sure to exercise tomorrow, and yet weeks go by without getting to the gym even once? If you have children, have you missed their soccer games, vowing to make it up next time? If you're in a partnership, do you miss dinners with your significant other and expect them to understand and accept your apology that work comes first—again? Are there friends you just can't seem to find time to reconnect with despite not visiting in months or years? Do you keep putting off medical checkups?

If this sounds like a typical day, week, month, year, or even decade, ask yourself, When was the last time you checked in with your spirit? If you're caught in a perpetually reactive work state with no time for intentional focus, it will lead to spirit loss. Chances are, like Caroline, you're not even aware it's happening. As the saying goes, it happens bit by bit and then all at once. One day you wake up to find that everything in your life has stopped working, except, paradoxically, work.

If you're caught in a perpetually reactive work state with no time for intentional focus, it will lead to spirit loss.

5 Csikszentmihalyi, *Flow*, 12.

I have seen this happen over and over to my colleagues. From the outside it looks as if spirits die without warning. But really, there are endless warning signs that we ignore. Often, we only slow down enough to act when burnout becomes impossible to ignore, usually because of a crisis like Caroline's chronic disease.

Catching burnout before it gets to this stage is crucial to salvaging your spirit.

SIGNS OF AN INTACT SPIRIT:

Evaluate your spirit and the spirits of others around you. A person with a healthy spirit

- exhibits vitality that seems to come from an inner fire,
- listens for the inner voice that tells them whether their actions resonate with their beliefs,
- connects to their spirit and vitality,
- brings their whole self to work,
- maintains a healthy amount of ego that stems from strength,
- stays "in integrity" and speaks truth even if it means not appeasing those who have the authority to fire them,
- prioritizes life and work activities and consistently reinforces boundaries to optimize both,
- keeps meaning and purpose intact, and
- focuses on relationships as much as tasks.

A PERSON WITH A DIMINISHED SPIRIT

- shows a loss of intuition;
- works harder but not smarter;
- is all motion and chaos;
- displays a loss of connection with their inner self and with others;
- loses touch with their hopes and dreams;
- exhibits a loss of energy;
- behaves from a place of negative emotions;
- acts out of sync with inner integrity, beliefs, and values;
- replaces all other relationships in life with work; and
- is reactive versus proactive.

If you were to check in with your spirit today, where would it be? Would it be intact or diminished?

What Destroys Spirit—and How to Get It Back

THE IMPORTANCE OF INTENTION

For Caroline, getting her spirit back began with paying attention to her everyday life. In other words she began to work with intention. Even when her typical day left her completely overwhelmed, she worked to build focus and awareness. She started by asking herself what it would look like to intentionally manage the barrage of incoming distractions: texts, chats, requests, and demands. To do this she began to look for what she called "energy patterns" in her calendar. When one day was intense, she made a point of making sure her next day was less intense.

To do this she had to learn that, as she puts it, "*No* is a complete sentence." Only when she intentionally built time into her schedule, free from distractions and constant stress from outside sources, was she able to find time for reflection, to focus deeply on the work that she truly cared about. She admits that it's still a constant challenge to carve out time for what she needs but says that she knows she must "vote for her well-being over the next chat or incoming text."

CREATING A NEW "GOOD"

The key to Caroline's recovery of spirit was deeper, however, than just simply saying no and scheduling away distractions. She also had to acknowledge that she had a deep-seated belief that "wisdom comes from pain." In other words she felt that her constant state of anxiety and depletion was *good.* Or, if not good, at least normal; thus, she shouldn't complain or give herself the break she needed.

When she switched her mindset to the idea that she could gain "wisdom from joy," everything shifted. She says that before she got well, she "lived by a sense of duty and overcare in all things." This played a hand in her constant multitasking, which created stress and anxiety and eventually contributed to her illness. Now she is "a lot more detached." Instead of this making her less effective, she found the opposite: "The only way to do my job really well is to be richly in touch with myself. The more in touch with my inner self I am, the more I am able to bring myself to my work."

That change did more than make Caroline healthier and happier. When she wasn't struggling under the constant anxiety of nonstop distractions, she was able to "send out" healing "care, appreciation, fun, and love" to her colleagues, creating a healthy work environment for everyone around her.

Caroline isn't alone in finding that saying no can be hard because of underlying beliefs. Robbie G., a software engineer, came to see that he was saying yes too much because "I was codependent on being the hero for people." He was the one who, as he put it, "always said yes."

However, after suffering loss of spirit and a resulting bout of burnout, he realized that trying to constantly attend to everyone else's needs meant that it "wasn't the best for the people I said yes to because they didn't get my full attention because I was spread so thin." Robbie learned to "say no to the things that I need to ... to ensure that I arrive to my workday with as much joy as humanly possible."

Of course, we can't just turn off our Teams chats and ignore emails. But even small adjustments help, especially when combined with the idea that we are acting for the good of everyone involved.

There is plenty of research on how multitasking doesn't work for us, but we don't need research to know what we experience at our jobs. How many times have you been on a work call when someone says, "Can you please repeat that?" This happens because we are all trying to be present in the Zoom meeting, reply to Teams messages, and accept calendar invites all at the same time. As Caroline and Robbie found, living this way can lead to overuse syndrome of the mind. Just like when we get physical overuse syndrome from sports, this overuse syndrome of the mind can eventually lead to burnout.

So what can you do?

The dilemma here is that to be incredibly effective in the corporation, your team members need to rely on you responding in real time—it is a professional code of honor, and it reinforces your integrity that you follow through, that you do what you say you are going to do. You cannot ignore the messages, but you can respond by letting others know you are on a call or working on a project, that you will get back to them as soon as possible so they are not left hanging—and then get back to them.

And like Caroline and Robbie, I have to remind myself that being reactive to every incoming signal is not a sign of a hard worker; it's a sign of a distracted worker. Learning to respond to the incoming signals based on priority is essential. I have to train myself to remember that my value is both in my immediate response when it is a priority and in the deep, good work I can contribute when I'm able to have the time to be in the present, connected to my work and my colleagues.

Seeking outside help can also be beneficial. For Caroline, this was a retreat with the HeartMath Institute. By adopting the HeartMath practices, Caroline learned a way to surf the waves of stress in the work environment and she specifically learned how to stop stress in the moment—which is a superpower because when we are able to de-stress in the moment, we are gaining more access to our brain cells. She was not only healthier and happier, but also able to create a healthier work environment by modeling work/life integration for all those around her.

The Roadblocks to Spirit-Keeping

In the coming chapters, we'll explore more ways that people lose their spirits and how they can get them back. The examples of Caroline W. and Robbie G. illustrate the first roadblock to holding on to spirit.

ROADBLOCK

Existing in a perpetually reactive work state, mistaking continuous and reactive activity for the deep work required to maintain our spirits

---

I will cover roadblocks to Spirit-Keeping, and we will work through them one by one. If that sounds daunting, I promise you that it is not only manageable but also deeply rewarding. The good news is that it is possible to hold on to your spirit and recover that inner fire, even if it's been out for many years.

CORE LESSONS CHAPTER ONE: BEING PROACTIVE

1. **Begin by building focus and awareness, even amid days that may leave you completely overwhelmed.**

   Imagine what it would feel like to be able to manage the incoming stream of meetings, chats, requests, and demands with attention and focus. Work toward that goal. Let your team and your peers know when you are blocking off deep work time during the day so they know you will get back to them as soon as you are done and break the cycle of interrupting yourself during this time.

2. **Get in touch with your work passions.**

   Allow yourself to revisit college visions of the mindset and passion you saw yourself bringing to a work environment. Schedule intentional time for those passions.

3. **Set aside time for deep thought.**

   Think about the last time you were able to enter consistent states of deep thought, where distractions were limited, and you had space and time to prioritize serious focus. In today's world applying this sort of deep thinking and deep work is nearly gone, and this is a loss for each of us. Remind yourself of the power of your creativity, knowledge, and satisfaction—all requiring intentional time to focus—that follow a job well done. Learning, or relearning, how to focus is a power that will never fail you. I would say that honing the skill to focus has been one of the keys to my personal success. Consider setting a timer for deep thought or tasks that you do not want interrupted.

4. **Ask yourself the following questions:**

- How would you define "spirit" in the context of your work life? How does this definition align with or differ from the common definitions?
- Can you identify any recent instances where you've experienced a state of "flow" in your work? How did it feel, and what conditions enabled it?
- Reflecting on the signs of an intact spirit versus a diminished spirit, where would you place yourself currently? What specific indicators led you to this assessment?

CHAPTER TWO

IT'S AN INSIDE JOB

Your internal values, passions, and goals

The best time to inspect the foundation is before you begin to build on it.

—ANONYMOUS

At one time in my corporate career, I led an executive leadership development program designed to identify and elevate high-potential employees.

This program wasn't just another item on my to-do list; it was a personal mission. When people asked me what I did, I'd say, "I work with people to help them assess their leadership competencies and provide them strategies, tools, and resources for their continued development to lead their organizations."

But my private answer was, "I reunite them with their spirits, the parts of them many have unknowingly checked at the door when they signed their employment contract."

I believe that one of the foundational leadership competencies is to know yourself, and the work of getting to know yourself is a journey of spirit. The journey is ongoing. It's hard work, but it results in being fully alive, productive, and engaged in all aspects of work and life.

To facilitate this journey for the people in the program, I hired a firm of psychologists. The goal was to offer something deeper than the standard corporate training; we wanted these individuals to delve into the very essence of who they were and what was important to them. Additionally, these sessions were designed to help the participants build self-awareness and understand their strengths and areas where they needed to improve.

These weren't ordinary coaching sessions. They were intense, introspective journeys and they were a significant financial investment in each individual. This significant investment wasn't just about the money. It was about the commitment to genuine, transformative growth. The psychologists conducted comprehensive 360-degree evaluations involving feedback from colleagues, friends, and family to paint a complete picture of the individuals' lives, both inside and outside of the workplace.

Leadership development programs like the one I was leading are essential for building a deep bench for the succession plan for any organization. A 2023 *Harvard Business Review* article showcased a study that included one thousand participants from around the world. It found that "under the right circumstances, leadership development can have a substantial positive impact on employees and employers. Specifically, these initiatives can drive personal growth, a clearer sense of self, greater meaning and purpose in life and at work, greater happiness, and reduced stress, ultimately enabling real transformation and a substantial boost in mental health and well-being. This in turn can foster improved engagement and effectiveness, empowering leaders to better support their teams and organizations."[6]

The first thing the program participants were tasked to do was to draft their personal vision. This proved to be the most challenging yet illuminating part for many participants. Most of them had never done anything like this before. They had no idea what their personal visions were. This phase was critical; it wasn't about assessing their performance as employees but helping them understand themselves as humans. What were their values? What gave them meaning? These questions were seldom asked within the confines of a corporate environment.

I considered the workshop a success when one of the candidates approached me, her eyes alight with a mix of fear and exhilaration.

"I worked through my personal vision," she confessed, "and I'm leaving."

This statement might make the program seem like a failure, but I was thrilled that this individual had discovered who she was beyond her job title. She realized that her path lay elsewhere, and that was a great outcome.

We can't all hire a team of credentialed outsiders to help us find our personal visions, nor should we, but the good news is, we don't have to. All it takes is a little introspection, time, and motivation.

A personal vision is made up of inner values, inner passions, and inner goals. Setting out to discover yours is the most important thing you can do to avoid burnout. Having an inner core and personal vision to help you navigate the challenges of the corporate world is nonnegotiable. The sooner you start, the sooner you'll have a clear grasp of how to save your spirit. Knowing your personal vision also

---

6 Ayse Yemiscigil, Dana Born, and Horace Ling, "What Makes Leadership Development Programs Succeed?" *Harvard Business Review*, February 28, 2023, https://hbr.org/2023/02/what-makes-leadership-development-programs-succeed.

helps separate your core identity from your work identity. This distinction is essential for holding on to your values and protecting your spirit when faced with the inevitable challenges of the workplace, such as reorganizations or layoffs.

Finding Your Values, Passions, and Goals

Your internal values, passions, and goals are the silent forces steering your life's journey. They are your compass in the corporate world, guiding you away from burnout and toward fulfillment. They're all related but slightly different.

Values are the foundations upon which we build our lives and careers. They are our deepest beliefs and principles that guide our decisions and actions. Values are what you stand for, regardless of the situation you find yourself in. For me, integrity, contribution, and growth have always been nonnegotiable. They dictate how I interact with colleagues, how I approach my work, and how I lead.

Passions are the fire in our belly. They are the activities, interests, or pursuits that bring us joy and satisfaction. My passion lies in unlocking potential in others, in transforming high-potential individuals into leaders not just capable of navigating the corporate maze but also thriving within it. This passion has led me to mentor colleagues—and to write this book!

Goals are the tangible expressions of our values and passions. They are what we aim to achieve, shaped by what we deeply care about. My goals have always been aligned with making meaningful contributions, be it through mentoring, developing future leaders, or advocating for diversity and inclusion in the workplace.

There is a whole industry of books written to help you find your personal vision. My favorites are not those about *how* to come up with a personal vision. Instead, they are inspirational and reflective books about how to create a life of meaning.

Here are some of my favorites:

- *Composing a Life* by Mary Catherine Bateson
- *Bird by Bird* by Anne Lamott
- *Man's Search for Meaning* by Viktor E. Frankl
- *The Second Mountain* by David Brooks
- *The Prophet* by Kahlil Gibran

Everyone will have their own list of books that speak directly to them. I advise asking friends and family for their lists of most meaningful books as a good place to start on the journey to find yours.

Here, I'll just offer a few thoughts to help you get started now to discover your inner values, passions, and goals. Embrace a willingness to ask yourself hard questions. Here are some simple ways to start:

1. **Reflect on your peak moments.**

   Consider the times when you felt most fulfilled and alive. What were you doing? Who were you with? These moments can provide insights into your passions and values.

2. **Seek feedback.**

   Ask close friends, family, and trusted colleagues what they see as your strengths and values. Often, they can offer perspectives you might overlook.

3. **Journal.**

Write about your experiences, thoughts, and feelings. Over time, patterns will emerge that highlight your core values and passions.

4. **Experiment.**

Try new activities, volunteer, or take on different projects at work. Exposure to diverse experiences can help clarify what you are truly passionate about.

5. **Visualize your future.**

Imagine your ideal life and work scenario. What are you doing? Who are you with? What impact are you making? This vision can help define your goals.

Embracing your values, passions, and goals isn't just about personal fulfillment; it's about bringing your whole self to your professional life. It's about creating a career that doesn't just exist on paper but one that resonates with the core of who you are. This alignment is the key to not just surviving but also thriving in the corporate world without losing sight of who you are as a person.

Inside versus Outside

One of the most defining moments in my career came a long time back when I was tasked with resolving a crisis so severe it threatened the very fabric of our corporate structure. The company's compensation system had imploded, a nightmare scenario where we couldn't pay our sales teams. Imagine the chaos—it was a disaster in the making.

The COO assembled a "tiger team" to tackle the issue, and I was chosen to be a part of this critical mission. The team was composed of a finance leader, a compensation leader, and a few other key players. We each brought a unique set of skills, problem-solving abilities, and perspectives to the table. The stakes couldn't have been higher.

It was the hardest problem I was ever asked to solve to this day. We worked tirelessly, sifting through complex data and outdated manual processes, looking for the fault lines that had led to this potentially catastrophic failure.

And we did it. We fixed the system. Against all odds, we managed to untangle the mess before anyone even knew that there was a problem. It was a tremendous relief, a moment of triumph that we all celebrated.

Following this success, I was offered a lead role in sales compensation. It was a significant promotion, a recognition of the hard work and dedication I had demonstrated.

I turned it down.

Why?

I knew I wasn't interested in the work. This decision, to some, might have seemed illogical. For me, it was a matter of integrity.

In my many years navigating the corporate landscape, I've encountered some people whose motivations could be distilled into two primary drivers: money and titles. These are the people who perceive every step of their career as a rung on a ladder leading to a higher salary or a more prestigious position. Ambition is not a flaw in itself, but when their lives are solely fueled by external rewards, it often doesn't end well. They chase the next promotion, the next accolade, not out of fulfillment, contribution, or internal growth, but for the veneer of success it offers. And even when they reach that next promotion, they still find they are not content.

In his book *Happier: Learn the Secrets to Daily Joy and Lasting Fulfillment*, author Tal Ben-Shahar called this phenomenon "the arrival fallacy."[7] He explains that personal improvement and ambition aren't bad per se, but when we get too caught up in future outcomes, we may grow attached to an unattainable level of perfection. When we can't reach that impossible peak, instead of being happy where we are, we continue setting higher and higher goals, hoping something will bring us joy. This creates self-doubt, as there are always new goals to take the place of those that have been achieved. We try to meet higher-revenue goals, finish a marathon, or become fluent in a new language. Achieving these goals can bring a temporary sense of happiness, but without a deeper, inner goal, the satisfaction quickly fades, leading to the pursuit of yet another goal and the potential for an ongoing sense of restlessness and unhappiness.

Commit to playing the long game by only evolving toward the roles and responsibilities that feed your spirit. Never stop asking for opportunities to engage with the areas of your work that bring you joy; plan for a three-to-five-year window to see real change. Careers and roles are not fixed boxes on an organization chart; they are more like circles with fuzzy edges that you can shape to expand or evolve. Creating and shaping your role to align with your inner values, passions, goals, and strengths is something only you can drive.

Inside or Outside: Beyond Work

To discern whether a value, passion, or goal is an inside job—one that feeds your spirit—or an outside job—primarily driven by external rewards—consider whether it can extend outside of your professional

---

7 Tal Ben-Shahar, *Happier: Learn the Secrets to Daily Joy and Lasting Fulfillment* (New York: McGraw-Hill, 2007).

life. For instance, if your passion is making the most money possible, anything you do outside of work is likely to fall flat.

Yet if your core value is to bring joy to others, cooking an amazing meal for a family gathering can be deeply fulfilling. If your core value is personal growth, finishing that marathon is a joyful, meaningful experience. These are the kinds of achievements that resonate with who you are beyond your job title or salary.

Inside values are marked by their ability to transfer to corporate life. This is why they're so important when it comes to avoiding burnout. One example is Manisha Arora, a Senior Director at ServiceNow. She discovered that her personal vision—striving to bring joy to others—isn't confined to her interactions with family, friends, and community.

She says, "I genuinely like the people I work with and make it my mission as a team lead to foster a sense of unity. We focus on building deep, personal connections, not through obligatory corporate activities but by genuinely caring about each other's lives."

Manisha's value of bringing joy to others not only enriches her family life but also allows her to avoid burnout by bringing that value into her work.

Inside or Outside: Who Are You?

Another test of whether you have discovered an inside or outside personal vision is to ask yourself, "If you lost your job tomorrow, who would you be?" This question isn't just rhetorical; it's a crucial reflection for anyone who is at risk of being too enmeshed in their work identity.

A different way of applying the Spirit-Keeper mindset to the question of who you are without your work was recently expressed by

Miley Cyrus in her 2023 Grammy acceptance speech for Record of the Year. In a room filled with applause and admiration, Miley, after receiving her award, said, "This award is amazing, but I really hope that it doesn't change anything because my life was beautiful yesterday."[8]

This struck a chord with me. It encapsulated a truth that extends far beyond the world of entertainment into the fabric of our daily lives, especially in the corporate realm: all the money, titles, and pats on the back will never change our inner core. We need to know our essence, who we are, and what we stand for. We are the same today as we will be tomorrow as we were yesterday, no matter how life happens around us.

In other words recognizing "inside" values means understanding who we are without our job titles and accolades. It's about knowing what sustains us when external validations are stripped away. You must foster values that aren't contingent on professional success but are intrinsic to your sense of self and fulfillment.

I listened to some of the other speeches given that night and found many similar sentiments expressed, including this one by Harry Styles, upon receiving his Grammy for Album of the Year:

> **"I don't think any of us sit in the studio making decisions based on what is going to get us one of these ..."[9]**

8 Recording Academy / GRAMMYs, "Miley Cyrus Wins Record of the Year for 'Flowers' | 2024 Grammys Acceptance Speech," February 4, 2024, YouTube video, 3:42, https://www.youtube.com/watch?v=L0x9pq6YijU.

9 Recording Academy / GRAMMYs, "Harry Styles Wins Album of the Year for 'Harry's House' | 2023 Grammys Acceptance Speech," February 5, 2023, YouTube video, 4:11, https://www.youtube.com/watch?v=Dbo1B9-0Q3Q.

I couldn't agree more. Here are some other personal visions I've heard from Spirit-Keepers. Is yours on this list?

- Continuing personal growth
- Building resilience
- Expressing creativity
- Appreciating life with gratitude
- Living in the present moment
- Cultivating joy
- Making a positive impact on the lives of others and the world

These values form the bedrock of who we are. They remain constant. When we hold the vision that resonates with us, if everything crashes down around us, we're still in touch with ourselves.

Inside or Outside: What Are You Talking About?

The final test to discern whether your personal vision is rooted in inner values or dictated by external metrics is simple yet revealing: stop talking about work outside of work. What then remains in your conversations? Do you find richness and depth, or does silence ensue?

When I entered the corporation and became my job, it was easy to become ensnared in my professional identity. Determined to avoid this pitfall, I cultivated interests and values that transcended my professional life.

The commitment to this broader vision became my guiding principle, ensuring that when I stepped away from the corporate arena,

I had a wealth of experiences and passions to fill my conversations and enrich my life. And when things went wrong at work, I still had things outside work that were going right. This approach transformed my interactions, making them more vibrant and multifaceted.

A Word on Passion

When I say that people must find their passion, what I mean is that they must find their inner passion, that thing they are passionate about that comes from inside them. Rarely, a person's inner passion can also be their career.

To me, the model of telling kids, "Go find what you love! Follow your passion," while inspiring, is a luxury reserved for those cushioned by wealth.

At seven years old, I discovered my natural affinity for oil painting. This early talent in the arts ignited a lifelong passion, yet I made the career decision not to go to art school to try to become a painter. Instead, I pursued Computer Science, recognizing its potential for financial stability.

Part of the reason I did this was the guidance from people I deeply respected, including a family member who was a successful artist. No matter his success, his advice was clear: "First, pick a career you can always fall back on."

This counsel wasn't meant to diminish my artistic passion but to ensure I had a secure foundation upon which to build my dreams. Computer Science promised reliability and independence.

The other reason I didn't follow my passion for art was that I have been working since I was eleven years old. That was when my parents got divorced, and I went to live with my mother, who held several jobs to make ends meet. I understood what it meant to not have financial stability, and I never wanted that for myself or my family.

However, don't misunderstand. Rejecting the pursuit of passion outright is not my message. Instead, I urge people to harmonize passion with pragmatism. I continuously seek avenues to infuse my work with creativity, be it through a creative approach to problem-solving, or storytelling, I try to find ways to marry my passion with my profession. It's about leveraging your strengths to ensure a stable future while also finding ways to weave passion into your work.

In any new role we take on in an organization, while we understand the responsibilities at a high level, we learn the specific day-to-day responsibilities of that role once we start doing the job. It is at this point that we discover the areas of responsibility in the role that we may be most interested in and that leverage our strengths. Once we discover these areas of interest and strength, the key is to build and shape our current and future roles around them. Make it clear to your manager the type of work you want to do more of that leverages your areas of interest and strength. Build your career over time around these interests and strengths.

I am constantly amazed and delighted to find that I'm not alone in this approach to a life-work-passion balance. A few of my fellow corporate tech warriors and I got together to form our not-quite-ready-for-primetime rock band, Liquid Code. Every member except for me brought years of musical experience, dedication, and passion from their lives outside of their day jobs. A couple of the band members have nurtured their musical talents for over twenty years while pursuing their day jobs in tech. The band, besides being one of the most fun experiences I have ever had at work, is a testament to how we all have many dimensions to our lives outside of work. We are tech workers by day and passionate musicians, artists, rock climbers, community leaders, painters, and so much more outside of our day jobs.

Let me pause here to note that for most of us, it is very hard to find time outside of work, especially when we also have family responsibilities. It sometimes seems impossible and can, in fact, be impossible at times to carve out any time for your passion. I know this—I live it. But I encourage you to try to carve out even a few minutes on weekends to keep your passion alive and to find your flow in your passion. It will pay off in the rest of your life and work.

The Reward of Inner Rewards

Throughout my career, I observed there were not many women leaders in tech organizations. And the few I saw move up, I saw move out pretty quickly. This observation wasn't just disheartening; it was also a clear indication of the uphill battle women faced in achieving and sustaining leadership positions in tech.

My experiences weren't unique.

- Women hold just 27 percent of tech jobs.
- A total of 11.3 percent of women in the tech and STEM spaces left the field in 2023.
- The percentage of women in all tech-related careers has actually decreased from 2023 to 2024.[10]

This situation has shaped my approach to work and success. My drive stemmed from internal competition and a deep-seated desire to

10 Jessica Hubbert, "70+ Women in Technology Statistics (2024)," Exploding Topics, accessed April 9, 2024, https://explodingtopics.com/blog/women-in-tech#sources.

contribute and excel, irrespective of the recognition that might come my way. It was my own internal competition with myself.

This mindset allowed me to navigate my career with a focus on personal growth, achievement, and contribution.

There will no doubt be times in your career when you may not be able to activate your internal drive for any number of reasons. When I have experienced these times, I have found it helpful to break the problem or the work project/initiative down into smaller and smaller parts and get very focused on delivering these smaller parts with the same care and work ethic as any other workstream.

When you find yourself in this situation, don't forget your past accomplishments and the transferrable skills you bring to the table. As the saying goes, "How you do anything is how you do everything." Building a strong work ethic will become an invaluable part of your work reputation. At the same time, focus on setting personal goals for yourself outside of work that support your daily motivation and give you the return of internal rewards.

When the Worst Happens

Sometimes, the rhetorical question of who you are without your job becomes a reality. One of the most difficult experiences in corporate life is getting laid off. Layoffs happen for many reasons—mergers, acquisitions, poor business results, strategic business restructuring where specific business units are shut down—and no matter the reason for a layoff, it can feel like a death. Anyone who has been through a layoff can relate to this. The suddenness of a layoff is devastating. It isn't just the loss of income that hits hard; it is the profound sense of void. I have had to lay off people and have also been laid off myself, and both of these experiences were very difficult.

When I was laid off, I learned a valuable lesson about the foundation upon which my values and goals were built. The ordeal forced me to confront and reevaluate what truly mattered to me beyond job titles and the corporate identity I had wrapped myself in. I found solace and strength in the inner values and goals I had cultivated. Those aspects of my being remained untouched, and I knew that my own internal drive would keep me going.

This introspection brought clarity and a renewed sense of purpose. I realized that my worth wasn't my job; it was rooted in my abilities, my resilience, and the contributions I could still make, regardless of my employment status.

Emerging from the experience of being laid off, I understood more than ever the importance of setting up one's values and goals. It's about knowing who you are and what drives you, independent of external validation. This profound realization is what allows us to survive and even thrive in the face of adversity.

Having a core is critical. It buffets you through really hard times. It helps you stay in the corporation, which then helps you financially. In the end, it's this inner strength, this unwavering sense of self, that carries us through life's most challenging moments.

ROADBLOCK:

Not having a personal vision made up of inner values, passions, and goals

CORE LESSONS CHAPTER TWO: FINDING YOUR PERSONAL VISION

1. **Recognize the importance of self-knowledge.**

   Understanding who you are beyond your professional identity is foundational. The journey is ongoing and it's hard work, but it results in being fully alive, productive, and engaged in all aspects of work and life.

2. **Engage in deep introspection.**

   The process of uncovering your personal vision demands deep introspection, often facilitated by feedback from those who know you in various capacities. Ask your partner, your family, and your friends to help you uncover what is important to you.

3. **Embrace the journey of discovery.**

   Understand that finding your personal vision is not a one-time task but a continuous journey of discovery and reevaluation.

4. **Identify your core values, passions, and goals.**

   At the heart of your personal vision are your values, passions, and goals. Remember the following:

- Values are the principles that guide your decisions and actions; they are what you deem important and nonnegotiable in life.
- Passions are the activities, interests, or subjects that deeply excite you and bring you joy.
- Goals are the objectives or outcomes you strive to achieve, shaped by your values and fueled by your passions.

5. **Embrace your uniqueness.**

   It's not about the expectations of others or the societal benchmarks of success. It's about aligning your work life with what truly matters to you, ensuring that your professional path and personal growth are in harmony. This alignment is what keeps your spirit intact and prevents burnout.

6. **Ask yourself the following questions:**

- What makes you feel most alive? Identify moments or activities where you lose track of time.
- What values do you find nonnegotiable, and how do they manifest in your daily life?
- What are your dreams and aspirations outside of your professional achievements?
- In moments of deep reflection, what do you wish for your legacy to be, beyond your career?

CHAPTER THREE

RELATIONSHIPS THAT NURTURE SPIRIT

Your managers, your reports, and your peers

Beginning in the late 1950s, a growing number of heretics emerged in … corporations. These were people within the firm who saw how … something desperately desirable had been lost in everyday corporate life: a sense of the value of human relationships and community.

—ART KLEINER, AUTHOR OF *THE AGE OF HERETICS*

At the beginning of my career, I was assigned a new manager. The first thing she told me when I first arrived on her team was, "My goal is to become vice president by the end of the year."

This person seldom gave any appreciation to anyone on the team. If the team wrote a report, the manager would take their names off and put her own on. If we did a great job on a project, we were lucky if we got a nod before we moved on to the next big challenge. The team felt undervalued and invisible.

I was right out of college and didn't completely understand how to recognize a harmful leader, much less how to extract myself from this manager. Almost by instinct, I started to assert myself more, making my contributions known and networking beyond my immediate team to build relationships with individuals who shared my values and work ethic. This proactive approach eventually led me to a new manager, someone incredibly appreciative and supportive.

This manager was confident in herself, a complete antithesis of my previous manager. When her managers said to her, "Good job!" she responded, "It wasn't me. It was the team." This experience underscored an essential truth about successfully navigating workplace relationships: it's not just about avoiding negative relationships but also actively seeking out and aligning yourself with positive people within the organization. Getting invited to join another team meant that other leaders had to know I existed, an insight that taught me the importance of visibility, not for the sake of recognition but for the opportunity to move within the organization.

In retrospect, navigating through this first challenging phase of my career was a rite of passage, offering me a clearer understanding of the type of leader I aspired to be. It reinforced my belief in the power of positive leaders, the value of genuine appreciation, and the importance of leadership that prioritizes the growth and well-being of team members. This experience taught me two of the most important skills needed to maintain your spirit in a corporation: **to form healthy relationships and avoid harmful ones**.

The following are three kinds of relationships in a corporation:

1. The relationship with your managers
2. The relationship with your peers
3. The relationship with your direct reports

All three matter if you want to keep your spirit intact.

Hierarchies in a Corporation

One aspect that sets a corporation apart from other forms of business is hierarchy. In a corporation, hierarchy is not just a characteristic but a foundational element that governs every area of daily life. Unlike in a start-up, where roles can be fluid and responsibilities often overlap, corporations are defined by clear tiers of authority and specialization.

Hierarchies bring benefits and challenges. On one hand they allow for large groups of people to work toward a common goal with efficiency and clarity of purpose. Each level of the hierarchy serves a specific function. This ensures that decisions are made in accordance with the organization's objectives and that the right people are in the right place to get the job done.

On the other hand, hierarchies can also introduce complexity, particularly when it comes to relationships. Climbing the ladder in a hierarchy can sometimes become a goal in itself. Competition among peers can poison the well. This is where politics come into play and where relationships can go very right—and very wrong.

Politics include power dynamics, alliances, and the strategic navigation of one's career. Where there's hierarchy, there's politics. I have worked with many people who are very good at their jobs—from engineers to data scientists to marketing experts to administrative assistants. They will say to me, "I just want to focus on my work. I just want to do a really excellent job. I don't want to get involved in politics."

Unfortunately, I have watched as many of these people lose their spirit or, worse, lose their jobs.

> **This highlights a crucial reality within corporate hierarchies: recognizing and navigating the inherent politics is not optional for those aiming to keep their spirits—or their jobs—intact.**

Positive Politics versus Negative Politics

There are two kinds of politics in a corporation: positive and negative, and you need to be constantly aware of both. This is a skill you will hone over time if you are early in your career, and it starts with awareness.

Positive politics are what make an organization a great place to work. The people who demonstrate positive politics are great team players. They give credit where credit is due, and you can rely on and trust them not only to achieve great results together but also to be there for you when you need them. You know that when you're not in the room, they're fully backing you and your work. It's all about an individual's character and trustworthiness. Striving to be a colleague who can be counted on and trusted—and identifying others in the organization who have the same goals you can team up with—helps keep your spirit and the spirit of the organization strong and flourishing.

Negative politics are used by people who are only out for themselves. There are specific characteristics that can tell you if someone is engaging in negative politics. They are always looking to make their next move in the organization, and on their way up, they'll ignore others without a thought. They may even be so blatant as to let you and anyone else know that their primary goal is to get their next promotion, and they generally have a reputation within the organization as a person who "only manages up." They take all the credit and rarely give it, including putting their name on others' work. You can never count on them to support you or your work when you are not in the room.

Maya Angelou has this great quote: "When someone shows you who they are, believe them the first time. They know themselves much better than you do."

SIGNS OF A POSITIVE MANAGER

Empowers and Trusts

A good manager gives employees autonomy, valuing their contributions and encouraging them to take ownership of their work. They delegate key projects to team members, encourage employees to set their own goals, and support team-led initiatives.

Promotes a Growth-Oriented Environment

Good leaders encourage learning and development. This manager provides opportunities for professional growth. They support your risk-taking and innovation. And they use failures as learning opportunities rather than reasons for punishment.

Acknowledges Contributions

Recognizing team members' efforts is crucial in a positive work environment. This manager finds ways to praise your achievements and the achievements of the team. They make sure you get promotions, raises, or other rewards for exceptional work. You can count on and trust them to advocate for your work when you are not in the room. When you are looking for your next opportunity in the organization, you can count on them to be your greatest reference to the next hiring manager.

Communicates Clearly and Openly

Effective leaders ensure everyone is on the same page and understands the bigger picture. This manager regularly updates the team on company news. They provide you with clear feedback on your work. They hold meetings or other avenues for your questions and comments.

Navigates Politics Positively

A positive manager uses their understanding of company dynamics to foster collaboration, not competition. They are not conflict averse, and they mediate conflicts to find win-win solutions. They mentor you in navigating workplace relationships. They are happy when you work across departments, recognizing this as an opportunity for your growth, not a threat to their power. You can trust them to have your back and support your work when you are not in the room.

SIGNS OF A SPIRIT-SAPPING MANAGER

Fails to Recognize and Appreciate

Every contribution under a spirit-sapping manager seems to vanish into thin air, with no appreciation, which fosters an environment of undervaluation. You stay until all hours and work through the weekend with merely a nod from your manager. Your team hits a major milestone, and there's no mention of thanks. After a standing ovation presentation, your manager takes the credit. Or they give the credit to their superiors, who have the power to accelerate their career.

Promotes a Fear-Based Culture

Instead of encouraging risk-taking and learning from mistakes, a poor manager instills fear of failure. This behavior significantly hinders innovation and personal growth. This type of manager publicly criticizes people in meetings. In a performance review, they focus solely on the negatives. If a manager yells, this is often a huge red flag. If you are constantly having to prove yourself, chances are, your spirit is being crushed.

Lacks Vision and Communication Skills

Good leadership thrives on clear communication and vision. A spirit-sapping manager often overlooks these, leaving the team directionless. You get conflicting instructions on a project, sowing confusion on who is responsible for what. You get feedback via rumor, not direct communication.

Has Poor Conflict Resolution Skills

A spirit-sapping manager is not only conflict averse but also unable to effectively manage conflicts, which can lead to unresolved issues, escalating a lack of productivity. Harmful relationships among team members are ignored. A poor manager asks team members to resolve their own conflicts so they do not have to get involved.

Bullies Their Team and the People around Them

You witness colleagues being publicly shamed or belittled for minor mistakes. The manager spreads rumors about team members or inappropriately shares personal information about team members, undermining trust and morale. If you feel dread at the thought of interacting with your manager, it's a clear sign of a bullying dynamic. This kind of mistreatment crushes the spirit and destroys team cohesion.

When You Have a Spirit-Crushing Manager

When you have a spirit-crushing manager, you must decide how you are going to deal with that person. In this situation you must align yourself with projects and leaders who are not spirit crushing, who are not in it just for themselves, and who are there to grow and encourage teams across the organization. The bad news is that this isn't always easy.

Throughout the years many people have told me that they just want to keep their heads down, do their work, and not pay attention or simply ignore the management dynamics and relationships above them. But I have also seen just as many times that people who hold this attitude—even as they're doing excellent work—discover that their contribution is overlooked when it's time to reorganize or cut head count. They are just as likely to be overlooked for the next promotion because no one knows they're doing excellent work.

An example of this attitude is the person who believes they are indispensable because they have always been the go-to person for solving major technical issues.

No one is indispensable. Every team member in an organization needs to assert themselves to ensure their contribution is known, while bringing the team with them at the same time and always giving credit where credit is due. It's a delicate balance, but it's crucial that your contribution and the contribution of the team are noticed if you want to keep growing in the organization.

Every team and group inside of a company has a culture. If the team and culture that you are in have negative politics, that won't help you thrive, and you'll be in danger of burnout. To make the move away from a negative culture, you and your accomplishments have to be visible to others outside your team. By forming strategic alliances outside your team, when there's an opening on another team, you'll be in a great position to go after that new role. You always want to have places to turn when you know it is time to move on—and it will be time to move on sooner or later, whether for career growth or for a better team culture.

When You're the Manager

As a manager, it is very important to know both your strengths and your weaknesses. Self-awareness is a crucial trait to being a great leader.

Another aspect of keeping your spirit intact as a leader is to remember that real success—and the increase in spirit that accompanies it—comes when everybody wants to work with you and for you because they can trust you, count on you, and rely on you. They know that you are always going to give credit to the team. People love to work with people who give credit because it feeds their spirit. On the flip side, people also love to work for people they know they can count on. If something goes wrong, they know the manager will take responsibility on behalf of the team and discuss what could have gone better in private with the team member or members.

How to Form Alliances outside Your Team

Most people in a corporation operate in a silo, with a focus on their local team. My advice to you is to work hard to get connected beyond your silo.

Work to extend your connections beyond your immediate circle. Connect with potential allies, engage with colleagues from different teams, and nurture relationships that transcend departmental boundaries.

These alliances become your lifelines, resources, and support systems, enabling you to navigate the complexities of corporate dynamics more effectively. You can move more easily when you are ready for that next career move because you will have established a robust network.

You can call on others outside your team for assistance, advice, or collaboration on a project. Or you can just have people to enjoy grabbing a virtual coffee with, significantly contributing to your ability to keep your spirit intact.

To do this, the first step is to accept or seek out opportunities to work with other teams.

If you're not able to find formal opportunities to work with people in other teams, you can still reach out to individuals you admire. Think about your three-to-five-year timeline: Whom do you see in a role that interests you? If you like that person's work style and the results they achieve, they're someone you should get to know. If you're experienced in your industry and are feeling burnout, who are the colleagues you know you can trust? Having someone to talk things over with makes a difference.

The first step is to identify who you want to connect with. Don't be afraid to ask for skip-level conversations. When you're in a company-wide meeting or on a big project, notice the people around you. I say to myself, *Hey, this person's really great at what they do. They're really excellent. I want to get to know them. I want to connect with them.* It takes work to form real relationships, so be sparing in your connections to ensure it does not take more and more time you may not have.

The second step is to establish credibility so people know that they can count on you. This is a critical survival skill, not merely a one-time event. For example, if someone needs help or has a question, I will try to help them immediately. I will try to answer as soon as possible, and if I am not able to get them an answer right away, I will always at the very least reply to let them know I see their message or their question, and I will get them an answer as soon as I can. I do this because I want them to know I see their request, and they can count on me to address it within a certain time frame.

For example, when I was leading a product tour, in just a few weeks, I enlisted the help of an amazing co-leader who was a strong team player and someone I could count on 1,000 percent. Then I engaged many other leaders who were executing efforts around the world. We were all operating as a team, yet we all reported to different organizations. It is critically important, when working in teams that span different organizations, to continually recognize the individual and team contributions back to the managers of those teams.

That's the kind of reputation and credibility in relationships that you want to form. It all comes down to integrity. You do what you say you're going to do, you follow through, and you do it every time. You ultimately end up being the person anybody can count on, and then, when you need something, you can also count on them.

Remember, though, you have to save your energy in the process. What I mean by "save your energy" is that you can eventually end up spending more time helping answer incoming requests that span far outside your role and responsibilities than you have time or energy for. You have to make the prioritization call on which of those requests will have to wait until you have time or until you can recommend another person to address the request.

Finding Mentors

A different relationship that can help shield you from burnout is the mentor relationship. Don't underestimate any formal mentoring and networking opportunities offered by your organization.

Personally, I have found informal mentoring relationships to be the most valuable. Finding informal mentors begins with recognizing the strengths in others and having the humility and curiosity to learn from them. Whether it's honing a specific skill or navigating the broader challenges of corporate life, reaching out for guidance has enriched my career in countless ways. When I see someone in a meeting or other work situation exhibit a skill I know that I lack, I reach out. I begin my ask with an acknowledgment of their skill. I might say, "I noticed in the meeting this morning how you handled conflict resolution with such poise. I'd love to learn from you. Do you think we could touch base once a month for an informal meeting? I'd love to run some of the situations I'm facing by you for your feedback."

Most people, when approached this way, are happy to help. Sally K., an extremely successful product manager, told me,

> Mentoring is a reciprocal journey. By participating, you're not just nurturing yourself but also paying it forward to others. So my resounding advice is to find that mentor or mentors early on in your career. Embrace those opportunities. And here, again, it can be difficult to find and make the time but even thirty minutes a month for virtual coffee. It's a transformative experience that fuels growth—for you and those fortunate enough to share the journey. I have been a mentor to others my entire career, and one thing that I did not expect is how much I would learn and do learn from my mentees.

Throughout my career I have been asked why I stayed so long at some of the organizations I have worked for. I always have the same answer: I feel like the luckiest person in the world to have worked for many of these companies because of the amazing people I get to work with every day, whom I learn from professionally and personally. These people are some of the smartest, kindest, most hardworking, most intelligent people I have known in my life. I am honored to work with them and call them my peers. Sometimes, these people show up when least expected to help give me guidance. I call these "mentoring moments." Do not think you have to find that "one" person to be your mentor. You can find amazing "mentoring moments" throughout your career as you find and form these wonderful work relationships that will help sustain your spirit.

Relationships among Peers

It's important to note that when you look for informal mentorship, your mentor can be a peer. In fact, some of the most rewarding mentorship relationships I've had are with my peers.

One example of a great peer mentorship I've experienced was when I first became a salesperson, and I shadowed the leading sales representative in the region. It's still crystal clear in my mind watching him interact with the customer. It was an amazing experience because he wasn't an in-your-face salesperson. All he did was ask questions, one after the other, to build on what he heard. If I had lacked the curiousity or had the attitude that I had nothing to learn from my peers, I would have missed his masterful lessons.

Paul F., a twenty-year veteran of the corporation and Spirit-Keeper extraordinaire, wrote this wonderful passage about his mentorship relationships with his peers:

> People ask why I think my job is awesome. I always answer truthfully—it's my team. I love the people I work with and for; they are smart, talented, and kind. The reality, though, is more nuanced. Lots of people have great teams and work on cool projects and products ... I revel in the fact that on my team, failure is seen as growth—we write about what we learned and try to share it with others.

When peer relationships are positive, it's wonderful. But not everyone on a team is worth your time and effort. The lessons of manager-report relationships hold in the case of peer relationships too. Don't let yourself burn out from relationships with peers who are not team players.

It is also essential that you make an effort to create a strong working relationship with your direct manager. You will work for every caliber of manager throughout your career, and if you find yourself working for a manager who is not a good manager, you need to start looking for your next opportunity to keep your spirit strong.

If You're Stuck

No matter how well you manage work relationships, there are times when the only way to save your spirit is to move on to another manager or a different department within your company or even to consider another corporation after first working to find a place to move within your current company. If this happens to you, don't beat yourself up over it. Just recognize the situation, and do what you need to do to save your spirit.

If you do everything in this chapter but still feel your spirit slipping away, it's possible that you work in a place that has systemic problems that you can't overcome. Not everything is in your control. Before you go somewhere else, it is important to investigate other areas in the organization where you can contribute. Consider doing this work anyway and doing it regularly, even if you are not ready to make a move. This way, you know what your next-move options are when the time comes. If there is nowhere else within your current organization, take your spirit somewhere else where it can revive and shine.

ROADBLOCK:

Spirit-crushing relationships that you must avoid to keep your spirit intact

CORE LESSONS CHAPTER THREE: NURTURING SPIRIT THROUGH RELATIONSHIPS

1. **Start by fostering genuine interest and curiosity about those you work with.**

   The foundation of any spirit-saving relationship in the workplace begins with a sincere interest in your colleagues' work and, from this, creating mutual opportunities for well-being.

2. **Dedicate time to nurture relationships.**

   Consider when you last took the time to develop a professional relationship without an immediate professional goal in sight. In today's fast-paced environment, the art of building and maintaining connections for their own sake is rare, yet it is crucial for a fulfilling work life.

3. **Take time to understand the difference between negative and positive politics.**

   Watch those around you and put them into categories. Learn from those who navigate in a positive manner and avoid the negative players. You'll encounter both positive and negative players in your career, and the quicker you can recognize what you're dealing with, the better.

4. **Ask yourself the following questions:**

- How do you currently engage with your colleagues across organizations? In what ways can you make more room in your schedule for meaningful conversations and interactions beyond the immediate demands of work tasks?

- Who do you trust in the workplace? Who do you admire? Who injects positive thoughts into your day? How might you reach out to these people?
- If your direct manager is negative, are you telling yourself that it's okay and you can manage? If so, what can you do to change your mindset and change the situation?

CHAPTER FOUR

KEEP YOUR (METAPHORICAL) BAGS PACKED

Standing up for yourself and others to keep your spirit intact

You've got to tell the world how to treat you [because] if the world tells you how you are going to be treated, you are in trouble.

—JAMES BALDWIN

Jane P., fresh out of college with a master's degree in data science, had just landed a significant role as a data scientist. Despite her qualifications and position, she found herself in an uncomfortable situation during a meeting with her colleagues.

As the meeting began, the leader introduced each team member. Jane was the only woman in the group. When he got to her, he chuckled and said, "And this is my notetaker."

Jane felt belittled. She knew that the others knew she was not the notetaker. After the meeting, she reached out to me.

I listened to Jane's story and immediately recognized the importance of addressing the issue right away. I advised Jane to send a message to the facilitator, stating clearly and assertively, "Your comment was not funny, and it was not acceptable."

Jane followed my advice. The facilitator's response was: "Oh, I didn't mean anything by that. That was not my intent. I'm so sorry. It was just a joke." I had already prepared Jane for this response and had suggested to her what her response should be.

She sent a follow-up email immediately: "The impact of your words matters more than your intent. Please don't make a joke like that again."

The Importance of Speaking Up for Yourself and Others

How do you respond to disempowering behavior in the workplace? Do you speak up or stay silent? The problem is, every time you don't do what you know is right, your spirit takes a hit. Nothing drives burnout faster than keeping silent when you know in your heart that you should speak up. One reason it's often hard to speak up is that we fear the consequences. We're afraid of losing our jobs or retaliation. This is why to keep your spirit intact, you need to keep your bags packed and ready to go.

I don't mean that literally. I only mean that you must have options if you find yourself in a spirit-draining work situation so you can consider the alternatives and choose what is right for you. Keeping your bags packed doesn't mean quitting. It's not about giving up. Far from it, it gives you the courage to do what you know is right. When you have a safety net and a plan B, you'll feel more empowered to address issues immediately. And save your spirit.

On the positive side, having your bags packed means that you'll authentically approach conflict in a way that's true to your inner spirit. When we're motivated not by fear but by a desire to create positive change, we create room for our spirits to grow. This mindset is only possible when we are willing to address and then, if necessary, move on, knowing that we have the resilience and resources to land on our feet. By keeping your bags packed, you're not planning to leave at the first sign of trouble, but rather you're ensuring that you have the strength and options to stand up for yourself and others when it matters most.

After Jane sent the message to the facilitator expressing her feelings about his inappropriate comment, she noticed a positive change in his behavior. The next time they were in a meeting together, he introduced her as the data scientist on the team. Jane felt a sense of relief and pride, knowing that her assertiveness had made a difference—maybe not just for her but for others too. But she didn't stop there.

When Jane experienced the inappropriate comment during the meeting at the start of her career, she hadn't yet developed the mindset of keeping her bags packed. She knew that her hesitation to speak up in the moment was rooted in fear. This fear had prevented her from standing up for herself and addressing the unprofessional behavior head-on.

Now she understood the importance of being prepared. Jane committed herself to start building her safety net, both financially and professionally. She began saving money, expanding her network, and investing in her skills and knowledge. By doing so she knew that the next time she faced a difficult situation, she would have the confidence and resources to speak up without fear holding her back. This was crucial not only for her well-being and growth but also for creating a more positive and respectful work environment for herself and her colleagues.

She had created a new tool in her tool kit for saving her spirit.

HOW TO PACK YOUR BAGS

Packing your bags, in the metaphorical sense of preparing for a potential career move, requires being ready for anything at any time. It could entail merely moving within your corporation to a new division or even just moving to a new manager. You need to think creatively. Here are some good places to start:

1. **Trust your instincts.**

   If you consistently feel the need to speak up, then there's probably something amiss in your situation, even if you can't put your finger on it. Prioritize your well-being and professional growth by being aware of how you feel and not just swallowing your feelings. If it doesn't feel right, it likely isn't.

2. **Start saving money.**

   Set aside a portion of your income, 20 percent, if possible, to build an emergency fund that can sustain you for a few months in case the worst happens and you lose your job. Obviously, this is easier said than done, but just having the goal often helps you to understand what you need.

3. **Continuously update your résumé and skills.**

   Regularly update your résumé to reflect your latest achievements, projects, and skills. Invest in your professional development by attending workshops, taking courses, or obtaining certifications relevant to your field.

4. **Keep in touch with your network.**

   Maintain relationships with colleagues, mentors, and professionals in your field. Attend industry events and engage in online communities to expand your network.

5. **Find the Spirit-Keepers.**

   Moving within your company is often the least disruptive option, so keep your eyes open for where people within your company have intact spirits, and then network with those people and groups. Finding the right environment where your ideal and real self can coexist might be right down the hall.

6. **Research other companies and opportunities.**

   Stay informed about other companies in your industry and the job market. Identify organizations that align with your values and goals, and keep an eye out for potential job openings.

How Not Standing Up for Values Erodes Your Spirit

When we fail to stand up for our values, we experience a profound sense of dissonance that gradually erodes our spirit. This erosion can manifest in various forms, from feelings of guilt and a loss of self-respect to a diminished sense of purpose. At its core the failure to uphold our values strikes at the very heart of our identity and integrity.

Psychologists have long recognized the importance of living in alignment with one's values. Carl Rogers, a prominent psychologist, has argued that incongruence between one's actions and their ideas of self leads to psychological distress. Rogers explains how every person has two selves.[11]

1. The real self is how we actually behave.
2. The ideal self is who we aim to be.

Being your authentic self and acting in accord with your values and actions can help prevent burnout.

Taking the risk to speak up is not trivial. It can lead to conflict—even potentially losing your job. Only if you're prepared for this can you take the risk of speaking up without an additional spirit-draining weight on your shoulders. Having your metaphorical bags packed can help give you the preparation and the courage to take the risk when you need to.

Standing Up for Others

Early in my career, I witnessed a situation that I couldn't ignore. I had a colleague, named Jeannie, who was the only female salesperson on one of the teams I had been working with. She was an outstanding salesperson and consistently exceeded her sales numbers. She was also gracious and wonderful as a human being to all she worked with, but despite her strengths, she was constantly being undermined and given uncalled-for negative feedback by her manager at every turn. Both Jeannie's sales peers and I observed the manager's behavior.

I could not stand by and watch Jeannie get negative public feedback she not deserve. I pulled the manager aside for a one-on-one conversation and told him what I had observed with specific examples of how he constantly praised others on the sales team but

11 Carl Rogers, *On Becoming a Person* (San Francisco: HarperOne, 1995).

did not acknowledge Jeannie's outstanding sales performance. I told him how it made Jeannie feel, that others had observed his behavior as well, that it was creating a negative team environment, and that this treatment was counter to Jeannie's exemplary sales performance.

My intervention made a difference. The manager's behavior toward my colleague improved, and she was able to continue her work without the public belittlement. She expressed her gratitude to me, acknowledging the significance of my support during that difficult time.

Looking back, I realize that my decision to stand up for my colleague was a turning point in my career. It reinforced my belief in the importance of speaking up and standing up for myself and others, even when it meant putting myself at risk. I felt empowered because I had my metaphorical bags packed. It was more important for me to stand up to injustice than to watch it happen, and I was prepared to be fired over that. This attitude has given me great confidence and strength in my career.

But I also recognize that not everyone has the same ability to stand up for themselves. Some individuals, because of their position, background, or circumstances, may not feel empowered to speak out against mistreatment. They may fear retaliation, job loss, or other repercussions that could jeopardize their livelihood.

In these situations those of us who have the strength and security to keep our bags packed need to use our voices for good. We must be willing to stand up for others who may not have the confidence to do so. By doing this we create a ripple effect of positive change, fostering a more inclusive and respectful work environment for everyone. And when we do that, unsurprisingly, our spirits soar.

Standing Up for the World

Kris Hansen, a chemist at 3M, made a startling discovery in 1997: PFOS, a fluorochemical produced by 3M, was present in human blood samples from the general population. Despite initially assuming her findings would be met with concern inside the corporation, Hansen faced skepticism from her superiors, who downplayed the potential harm of PFOS, a man-made compound not meant to be in human bodies.[12]

Hansen stayed at 3M for twenty-six years, shifting her focus within the company after her findings were largely dismissed. She found herself ostracized, and so she moved teams and avoided the subject of fluorochemicals for nearly two decades. Hansen felt sure her knowledge of the situation had tainted her professional life. In October 2022 her job was eliminated, and she chose not to apply for a new one. By this point Hansen had read independent studies linking PFOS and PFAS, the more general classification of "forever" fluorochemical of which PFOS is a subset, to health issues such as developmental and immune-system problems.

In 2022 Hansen finally decided to speak out about the silence she had witnessed inside 3M. When asked why she waited so long to speak up, she told a journalist at the *New Yorker*, "You've got literally the medical director of 3M saying, 'We studied this, there are no effects.' … I wasn't about to challenge that … It almost would have been too much to bear at the time."[13]

But there were effects. PFOS and PFAS enter our cells and organs, interfering with basic biological functions. The *New Yorker* explains,

---

12 Sharon Lerner, "How 3M Discovered, Then Concealed, the Dangers of Forever Chemicals," *New Yorker*, May 20, 2024, https://www.newyorker.com/magazine/2024/05/27/3m-forever-chemicals-pfas-pfos-toxic.

13 Lerner, "3M."

"New health effects continue to be discovered. Researchers have found that exposure to PFAS during pregnancy can lead to developmental delays in children. Numerous recent studies have linked the chemicals to diabetes and obesity. This year, a study discovered thirteen forever chemicals, including PFOS, in weeks-old fetuses from terminated pregnancies, and linked the chemicals to biomarkers associated with liver problems. A team of N.Y.U. researchers estimated, in 2018, that the costs of just two forever chemicals, PFOA and PFOS—in terms of disease burden, disability, and health-care expenses—amounted to as much as sixty-two billion dollars in a single year. This exceeds the current market value of 3M."[14]

Hansen, of course, wasn't the only one who knew the harm. Many in the organization did, including her direct manager, who kept so quiet that he didn't even tell Hansen what he knew, even when she made the discovery too.

Hansen's story underscores the importance and the difficulty of speaking out. These two chemists, among many others, knew about these chemicals for decades and did not push to take their knowledge forward. Now studies show that 99 percent of all humans, including fetuses, have measurable levels of PFAS in their bloodstream as a result.[15] This is an example of when following one's personal ethics and finding allies are critically important. Choosing to remain silent in this sort of situation led to more than a loss of spirit—it led to a global health crisis and may still lead to the destruction of the

---

14 Lerner, "3M."

15 "99 Per Cent of Humans Have PFAS Chemicals in Their Blood," ChemSec, accessed June 14, 2024, https://chemsec.org/wrappedinchemicals/facts/pfas-fact-1/#:~:text=The%20industrial%20use%20of%20PFAS,effects%20on%20the%20immune%20system.

company. As of 2022 more than sixteen thousand of 3M's products still contain PFAS.[16]

It's easy to judge Hansen and her colleagues for not speaking up sooner. Many of us are fortunate enough to never face such weighty ethical dilemmas in our careers. While we hope to never find ourselves in such a situation, Hansen's experience serves as a reminder of the importance of speaking out and how having our bags packed makes it easier to do the right thing.

Navigating Career Shifts with Resilience

When you find yourself at a crossroads in your career, whether due to a choice you made to seek growth, uphold your principles, or because of external circumstances, it's natural to feel a mix of emotions. Fear, anxiety, and self-doubt may creep in, causing you to question your decisions and prospects. However, it's crucial to remember that change, even when unexpected, can be a catalyst for positive transformation and an expansion of your spirit.

Embracing the unknown requires a shift in perspective. Instead of viewing the career shifts that standing up for yourself and/or standing up for others can lead to as setbacks, try to see them as opportunities to explore new paths and expand new horizons. This mindset allows you to approach challenges with curiosity and openness rather than resistance and fear. By staying receptive to new possibilities, you may discover hidden talents, passions, or career directions that you had never considered before.

In other words you need to cultivate resilience. Resilience is the ability to bounce back from adversity, adapt to change, and maintain

16 Lerner, "3M."

a sense of purpose and optimism in the face of challenges. Building resilience involves the following key strategies:

- **Reframe Changes as Learning Opportunities**

  Look for the lessons and growth potential in every challenge you face. Ask yourself, "What can I learn from this experience?" and "How can I use this knowledge to improve myself and my career?"

- **Maintain a Support Network**

  Surround yourself with positive, supportive people who believe in you and your values. Lean on your network for encouragement, advice, and guidance during times of transition.

- **Practice Self-Care**

  Taking care of your physical, mental, and emotional well-being is crucial during periods of change. Engage in activities that bring you joy, reduce stress, and help you maintain a balanced perspective.

- **Celebrate Small Victories**

  Acknowledge and celebrate the progress you make along the way, no matter how small. Recognizing your achievements can boost your confidence and motivation, helping you stay focused on your goals.

- **Embrace a Growth Mindset**

  Believe in your ability to learn, grow, and adapt. Embrace challenges as opportunities to develop new skills and knowledge rather than as threats to your success.

Remember that your values and principles are the foundation upon which you build your professional and personal life—and your spirit. When you stay true to yourself and remain open to change, you'll find that your spirit not only survives but also thrives, even in the face of adversity.

ROADBLOCK:

Not standing up for yourself and others

CORE LESSONS CHAPTER FOUR: PACKING YOUR BAGS

1. **Speak up for yourself and your values.**

   When faced with disempowering behavior or situations that compromise your values, it's crucial to speak up and address the issue head-on. Staying silent may lead to the erosion of your spirit and contribute to burnout.

2. **Be prepared for unexpected career shifts.**

   Having your metaphorical bags packed means being prepared for potential career changes, whether within your current organization or elsewhere. Build a strong foundation of skills, networks, and financial stability to navigate these shifts with resilience.

3. **Stand up for others when necessary.**

   If you witness mistreatment or injustice toward colleagues who may not have the power to speak up for themselves, use your voice to support and protect them. This creates a ripple effect of positive change and fosters a more inclusive work environment. It is often best to speak to the person you are standing up for before you lean in to help them to ensure they are supportive of your assistance.

4. **Cultivate resilience and adaptability.**

   Embracing unexpected career shifts requires a mindset of resilience and adaptability. Reframe challenges as opportunities for growth, maintain a support network, practice self-care, celebrate small victories, and believe in your ability to learn and grow.

5. **Ask yourself the following questions:**

- Do you consistently speak up when faced with situations that compromise your values or make you uncomfortable at work? If not, why not? Can you think of times that you wish you had? What had stopped you?
- Are you actively building a financial safety net to support yourself in case of unexpected career changes?
- Are you prepared to stand up for your colleagues who may be facing mistreatment or discrimination?
- Are you cultivating a mindset of resilience and adaptability to navigate unexpected career shifts? Have you developed a plan to prioritize your well-being and maintain a healthy work-life balance, even during times of change?

CHAPTER FIVE

DON'T BE NUMB TO BEING HUMAN

Emotions and boundary building in the workplace

What we don't need in the midst of struggle is shame for being human.

—BRENÉ BROWN, PROFESSOR, AUTHOR, AND RESEARCHER

I have learned through my forty years in a corporation that we can't simply ignore our emotions when we walk into the office. We can't compartmentalize ourselves and pretend that the outside world doesn't affect us. When something significant happens, such as the start of a war, a death in the family, the birth of a new baby, a divorce or separation, or even just a big win at your weekend softball tournament, it touches us because we are all human.

However, I have also learned that there are appropriate ways to bring emotions into the workplace. We can't let our feelings consume us or disrupt our work, but we can acknowledge them and create spaces for compassion. It's about finding a balance and being professional while still honoring our humanity.

We don't have to check our emotions at the door, but we do need to find healthy ways to express them.

Whether it's simply acknowledging the impact of world or personal events, we can create a workplace culture that values both productivity and emotional well-being. It's not about ignoring our feelings but rather learning how to relate to them in a way that brings us closer together and reminds us of our shared humanity.

The Trouble with Repressing Emotions at Work

It's easy to fall into the trap of believing that emotions have no place in the workplace—whether positive or negative. We're often told to "leave our personal lives at the door" and to "be professional" at all times. While it's true that we need to maintain a certain level of professionalism at work, completely suppressing our emotions can have serious consequences.

When we're unable to acknowledge and process our feelings, they don't simply disappear. Instead, they can manifest in unhealthy ways, such as irritability, anxiety, or even physical symptoms. Over time, this emotional repression can lead to burnout, disengagement, and a general sense of dissatisfaction with our work and our lives.

Moreover, when we pretend that everything is always "fine," we miss out on opportunities to connect with our colleagues on a deeper level. We may fail to offer support to someone who is struggling or to receive support when we need it ourselves. This lack of authentic connection can make us feel isolated and alone, even when we're surrounded by people.

The solution is to use discretion. It takes a toll on the spirit to suppress our feelings entirely. It's also inappropriate to unload most of our personal problems on our colleagues or allow our emotions to interfere with our work. Instead, we need to find a balance—a way to acknowledge and manage our emotions in a professional, constructive manner. By finding this balance, we can not only avoid losing our spirit but also tap into a powerful source of motivation, connection, and fulfillment in our careers.

Life is filled with difficult and inevitable life events, celebrations, loss, and change. As you and your team members face these events, it is important to connect at the human and deeper personal level. While you may already do all of these things naturally, here are a few high-level reminders for connecting more personally at work:

1. Share significant events with your most trusted colleagues.
2. Be there for your most trusted colleagues, and depending on the situation, express sincere congratulations, your support, or your condolences.
3. If the situation is a personal loss or tragedy, check in with your colleague over time to let them know you are there for them and thinking about them. Send flowers and extend an offer to help.
4. If the situation is a celebration, send your own personal congratulations and a gift.

If you find the "emotional norms" of your workplace conflict with what you are comfortable with, you might want to consider alternative places to work. To be your authentic self, and not burn out or lose your spirit, you need to ensure that you're working at a place where you can be authentic.

Understanding the Emotional Culture of Your Workplace

Every organization has its own unwritten rules around emotional expression, and learning to read these cues can help you maintain professionalism while still being authentic.

You can learn these rules by observing how your colleagues express their emotions. Are they generally reserved or more expressive? In many workplaces negative feelings are discouraged, while positivity and optimism are emphasized. In others openly showing grief or discussing illness can be seen as a sign of weakness.

Your role and position within the company can also affect how you express emotions. If you're in a leadership position, you may need to set an example of emotional regulation for your team. If you work closely with clients or customers, you may need to maintain a specific emotional demeanor to represent the company. On the other hand, if you're part of a team that values emotional intelligence and empathy, you may have more leeway to express your emotions authentically.

For example, after the tragic death of one of our colleagues, another colleague, Paula, created what she called a compassion session. It was a place for people to be together and grieve over the loss of our friend. Paula held a virtual meeting and opened it up to anyone who wanted to attend. She acknowledged the tragedy that had occurred and asked everyone on the call to take a moment of silence and send compassion to our colleague's family. It was a way to acknowledge the human suffering and the grief we all felt and sit with it in silence with others while sending comfort and compassion to the family who was impacted.

Guidelines for Hosting a Compassion Session:

- Identify the unwritten rules around expressing specific emotions.
- Observe and adapt to the emotional norms of your specific workplace culture.
- Consider how your role and position may impact your emotional expression.

Emotions across the Globe

Navigating the expression of emotions in international cultures at work can also be a complex and delicate task. It requires a keen awareness of cultural differences, the ability to adapt your own emotional expression, and the skill to observe and mirror the emotional expression of your colleagues. Of course, there are exceptions to any broad statement of cultural norms, but having emotional intelligence means paying attention and adjusting to your surroundings.

Having worked with teams all over the world, I've found that in many places, strong emotion is especially discouraged. For example, I've observed that in many Asian cultures, maintaining a calm and controlled demeanor in professional settings is highly valued. This emotional regulation has been shown to be especially valued in the case of expressing negative emotions.[17]

In other cultures, such as Germany or Scandinavia, I've found that people can be extraordinarily direct and to the point, even when expressing strong emotions such as criticism or disagreement. This can come across as harsh to those from cultures that value more indirect communication. In some Latin American cultures, I've found that expressing emotions openly and enthusiastically is more common, so showing more warmth and passion in your interactions can be beneficial.

Diversity and Workplace Emotion

Emotional labor, a term coined by sociologist Arlie Hochschild in her book *The Managed Heart*, is the idea that regulating one's emotions to meet workplace expectations takes work akin to physical labor. If that work isn't understood, acknowledged, and limited, it can lead to burnout. This kind of burnout is especially at risk in public-facing jobs. Salespeople, for example, are often expected to always be upbeat, and that can take a toll on their spirit.

As the Weld Lab for Workplace Emotional Labor and Diversity at Penn State University reports, "Emotional labor, like physical labor, is effortful and fatiguing when done repeatedly all day long and can be costly in terms of performance errors and job burnout."[18]

In this way emotional labor disproportionately affects members of underrepresented groups because of the constant need to navigate and conform to majority expectations. Self-monitoring and regulation

17 "Cultural Differences and Rating EI," Sigma Assessments Systems, accessed June 15, 2024, https://www.sigmaassessmentsystems.com/ei-and-culture/#_edn4.

18 Pennsylvania State University, "What Is Emotional Labor?" Workplace Emotional Labor and Diversity, accessed May 12, 2024, https://weld.la.psu.edu/what-is-emotional-labor/.

can be taxing on psychological and emotional resources. As explained in a report by the American Council on Education,

> **Those with more power are able to express emotions in different ways than those who are more marginalized, and emotions are interpreted differently by those with different identities and experiences, which gives political weight to emotions.**

For example, emotions such as anger or sadness that may be seen as negative by those with privilege may actually serve an important purpose when they are felt or experienced around issues of oppression and inequity. One could argue that we should feel angry when confronted with injustice, and we should feel sad when students or colleagues share painful stories of racist experiences.[19]

In other words there are some conditions in which expressing strong emotion at work is healthy and necessary to avoid burnout.

For underrepresented employees, emotional labor often includes the additional burden of managing the stress of potential biases or stereotypes. Many feel the pressure to adjust their emotions to fit into the prevailing corporate culture, avoiding any display that could reinforce negative stereotypes.

Thus, the emotional labor for under-represented group members is not just about the expression of workplace emotions but also about the suppression or careful curation of identity. The constant strain to express "normal" or "acceptable" levels of emotion according to

---

19 Darsella Vigil et al., "Emotional Labor in Shared Equity Leadership Environments: Creating Emotionally Supportive Spaces," American Council on Education, accessed June 15, 2024, https://www.acenet.edu/Documents/Shared-Equity-Leadership-Emotions.pdf.

majority standards can lead to a sense of inauthenticity, further exacerbating the risk of burnout.

How to Offset Emotional Stress

One person I interviewed for this book told me, very wisely, "Don't get emotionally attached to work's ups and downs. Enjoy the highs, but recognize they are temporary, and the lows will pass. Understand that fluctuations in your career trajectory are natural and not permanent."

Of course, emotional detachment is easier said than done.

HERE ARE A FEW TIPS FOR REGULATING EMOTION:

- **Choose Your Battles**

  Not every situation warrants a full-fledged emotional response. Sometimes, it's best to pick your battles and let go of minor irritations.

- **Identify Your Triggers**

  Recognize what situations or behaviors tend to evoke strong emotions. Are there specific meetings or types of interactions that consistently leave you feeling frustrated? Once you're aware of your triggers, you can start to develop coping mechanisms.

- **Take a Breath**

  It can be tempting to react impulsively in the heat of the moment. Instead, try to take a step back and take a few deep breaths. This will give you some space to process your emotions and respond in a more measured way.

- **Know When to Walk Away**

  If you feel yourself getting overemotional, consider giving yourself a day to reflect before you respond. It might be best to table the conversation or fire off an email and come back to it later when you've had a chance to cool down.

Remember, setting boundaries isn't about bottling up your emotions or becoming robotic. It's about protecting your well-being and ensuring you express yourself in a way that is professional and productive.

Setting Boundaries

You have to have boundaries. Especially in moments of vulnerability, you must carefully manage what to share and with whom. It's okay to show emotions at work, but only with those you truly trust. You have to understand who really cares.

In an article in the *Harvard Business Review* titled "The Toxic Effects of Branding Your Workplace a 'Family,'" author Joshua A. Luna points out a crucial but subtle distinction when deciding how to share vulnerabilities at work. He writes that businesses work better when there's a culture not of "we're all in this together" but rather "we share the same purpose." This very slight difference helps when setting clear boundaries and accepting the professional nature of work relationships.[20]

20 Joshua A. Luna, "The Toxic Effects of Branding Your Workplace a 'Family,'" Harvard Business Review, October 27, 2021, https://hbr.org/2021/10/the-toxic-effects-of-branding-your-workplace-a-family.

Boundaries for When You're in Crisis

I have seen many people in the workplace share beyond their trusted colleagues and endure a lack of support from others. It's a fine line. While you should be able to share with trusted colleagues, there are still crises you may want to consider not sharing.

We are all dealing with something, and we all have personal challenges and struggles. For example, we may have just suddenly lost a family member, we may be pregnant, or we may have a chronic autoimmune disease. We should be able to discuss these things and be supported by trusted colleagues, and we should, in turn, provide that support to others. We are with our work teams every day of our lives, so we need to be able to be human and be real. And when we work in organizations where leaders share their own personal challenges, this also helps everyone because it serves as a role model for others.

While it's important to be authentic at work, it's also important to use discretion. Oversharing can make it difficult for you to separate your work identity from your personal struggles, which can lead to emotional strain and a loss of spirit. There is a fine line in what you may want to share. While you should be able to share with trusted colleagues who have your best interest in mind, there are still crises you will want to consider not oversharing.

Here are four examples of crises you might not want to share at work:

- **Financial Problems**
- **Mental Health Issues**
- **Addiction**
- **Family Conflicts**

It's important to have a support system outside of work, whether it's family, friends, or a professional therapist. These are the people with whom you can be fully transparent and who can offer you emotional support.

In the end it's about striking a balance. It's important to be human at work, but it's also important to be strategic about what you share and with whom. By setting clear boundaries and being selective about sharing personal crises, you can protect your emotional well-being and maintain your professionalism.

For example, if you have a visible physical disability, it's not something you can or should hide. However, you can choose how much detail you share about your condition and how it affects you emotionally. You might inform your colleagues or supervisor about any accommodations you need and be cautious about who you share the emotional ups and downs with.

If you're dealing with a serious illness or family emergency that requires extended time off, again, you'll need to inform your workplace. But you can do so in a way that focuses on the practical implications, such as your expected return date and any work contingency plans, rather than the emotional toll it's taking on you.

I had a manager some time back who suffered from serious depression. He would take off when necessary and then would return when he was ready with a simple statement that he was back. That felt very appropriate, and we all admired him for his honesty and his boundaries. He followed these basic steps I advise for all such situations:

- Separate the practical from the emotional and share only what is necessary for your colleagues and managers to know in order to support you and ensure business continuity.

- Don't feel obligated to share the deeply personal emotional journey unless you feel safe and comfortable doing so with your most trusted colleagues.

Remember, it's not about being inauthentic or hiding your humanity. It's about managing your emotional labor and protecting your vulnerability in a professional setting. By focusing on the practical aspects and saving the emotional processing for your trusted colleagues at work and your support system outside of work, you can navigate these challenging situations while maintaining your professionalism and preserving your emotional well-being.

ROADBLOCK:

Not finding healthy ways to express your emotions at work and not setting up emotional boundaries

CORE LESSONS CHAPTER FIVE: BRINGING YOUR HUMANITY TO WORK

1. **It's important to acknowledge your emotions at work and to find trusted colleagues with whom you can share these feelings while at the same time doing so in a manner that respects professional boundaries.**

   Suppressing emotions at work can lead to burnout, disengagement, and loss of spirit. Oversharing can lead to making others uncomfortable. Thus, it's important to set clear boundaries for yourself, share with your trusted colleagues, and use discretion.

2. **What your specific boundaries are depends on your workplace culture, your role within the organization, and other cultural differences.**

   Where you're from, your identity, your role, your specific company, and so on create a unique situation in which you need to think deeply about where to draw the line between sharing and oversharing. For example, a manager may need to maintain more emotional distance than an entry-level employee, or a salesperson in a high-energy start-up may have more leeway for emotional expression than an accountant in a traditional firm.

3. **Salvaging your spirit depends on having outside resources for expressing the emotions that are inappropriate at work.**

   Family, friends, therapists, support groups, hobbies, and creative outlets are all important resources for processing and expressing the full range of your emotions outside of work. By having these outlets, you can maintain your emotional well-being and bring your best self to work—including all the appropriate emotions—without burdening your colleagues or risking your professionalism.

4. **Ask yourself the following questions:**

- How can you adapt your emotional expression to different cultural contexts while remaining true to yourself?
- Do you have emotional triggers in the workplace? If so, do you have effective ways to address them?
- Can you make a list of three to four people you can trust with your personal emotional struggles at work? If not, how can you identify possible candidates you can trust?

CHAPTER SIX

LISTEN TO YOUR BODY

Let me be one of the harbingers that lead you to the mysterious core of your being where insight and wisdom are naturally available when called upon with a sincere heart.

—KAVERI PATEL

Shelby Wolfe had just begun her corporate career when the opportunity arose to attend a ten-day silent Vipassana meditation retreat. She had always been curious about connecting with her spirit and was committed to balancing her corporate career with her spirit-nurturing practices. The specific retreat taught the technique of Vipassana, which was developed by the Gautama Buddha over 2,500 years ago. According to Buddhist tradition, the Buddha attained enlightenment after meditating under a bodhi tree for forty-nine days. Vipassana, which means "to see things as they really are,"[21] is a method of self-transformation through self-observation and introspection.

Shelby went in with an open mind and without expectations. At the same time, she acknowledged, "I think something that I couldn't let go of was that I did hope to know myself better, understand myself better, and maybe bring some of what I learned back into my everyday life."

For ten days, Shelby sat in stillness and silence for up to ten hours each day. The physical pain and discomfort were intense at first.

"You're sitting day after day with your body completely still and in a cross-legged position. To sit like that for a long time creates a lot of pain in your body—both big sensations like muscle cramps and smaller irritations like wanting to scratch an itch," she reflected.

As taught in the training, she would systematically scan her body from head to toe, inside and out. Shelby began to notice the subtler sensations underneath the bigger, more painful ones.

"The practice itself is to go through every square inch of your body, from your head to your feet and back up and back down as slowly as possible, to become extremely aware of every sensation that you feel within your body. You're supposed to be aware of the subtlest sensations possible, so the tiniest tickles or the vibrations of your molecules, while you're also experiencing pain and bigger sensations."

She realized that by observing her body's sensations with equanimity, without reacting to the pain and discomfort, she could find a place of inner freedom and peace.

---

21 Ala'Aldin Al-Hussaini et al., "Vipassana Meditation: A Naturalistic, Preliminary Observation in Muscat," *Journal of Scientific Research in Medical Sciences* 3, no. 2 (October 2001): 87–92, https://www.ncbi.nlm.nih.gov/pmc/articles/PMC3174711/#:~:text=Vipassana%2C%20which%20means%20to,and%20self%2Dawareness%20through%20meditation.

"We are constantly reacting to pain and itches and things that we can feel, but there's also stuff that our body is going through under the surface that our subconscious mind is aware of that our conscious mind is not. So the practice sharpens a subtle awareness of your body and space, not to ignore your pain but to understand how you react to the bigger sensations versus the smaller sensations and to develop a sense of awareness and ability to listen and also equanimity to being nonreactive to those bigger, more painful sensations so that you're able to become even more aware of the subtler sensations."

Shelby left the retreat with a newfound appreciation for her body's innate wisdom and the mind-body connection. When she returned to work, she found simple ways to integrate the practices. Since she came back, she says she's been "taking a lot more time to check in with myself before work and throughout the day. I get up and walk around—very simple things to ensure that my body feels centered, and I don't get too far away from my body." She realized that mind-body awareness "retrained my mental patterns to feel more connected with the present moment that my body is in."

The Mind-Body Connection

We can't all go on a ten-day silent meditation retreat and many of us would not want to. But Shelby's story can still teach us a lot about losing our spirits in the workplace because ironically, what we do at work every single day is the same thing Shelby did at her retreat: sit for hours and hours. The difference, of course, is that we ignore our bodies. We push ourselves to sit in front of screens, skipping meals, sacrificing sleep, and powering coffee, not in the name of insight but in the name of productivity. Over time, instead of creating a connection to our bodies, we create dissociation.

Why does this matter, and what does this have to do with keeping our spirits intact?

When we ignore our body's needs, our physical and spiritual health suffer. We suffer physically because stress can lead to disease, as we saw in the story of Caroline W. in chapter 1, the woman who found herself on the speaker's stage, unable to stand. We suffer spiritually because when we lose access to the body's intuitive wisdom, creativity, and joy, we start to feel that we are just "cogs in the machine," working to live while our sense of purpose and connection to ourselves and others withers.

The solution is both simple and profound: we must learn to listen to our bodies again. This is not always easy, especially when workplace culture glorifies pushing yourself to the limit. It takes willpower and conscious intention to prioritize our physical well-being in the face of endless demands on our time and energy. But it is an act of courage, self-love, and faith that when we take care of ourselves, we are better able to thrive and serve in all areas of our lives.

What are our bodies' basic needs, and how can we listen to them? The four core physical needs are nutrition, movement, rest, and relaxation. We need them all in order to save our spirits.

Nourishing Your Soul

Let food be thy medicine.

—HIPPOCRATES

During a busy workday, how often do we actually pay attention to what we're eating? I often find myself at lunch in front of my computer trying to power through one project or another. I have no idea what I ate. I don't know how it tasted. I don't have time for all that.

Being connected to what we eat isn't easy. To take the time to actually eat and be with the food that we're eating and understand what we're eating takes time that we don't feel we have. It takes willpower to reconnect to our food. When we're so disconnected from our food, we don't get any pleasure from it, putting us at risk of losing our spirits.

This mindless eating takes a toll not just on our physical health but also on our overall well-being.

- **Listen to your mother.**

  My mother always said *you are what you eat.* I believe this is true. Every bite you eat should nourish your body and your spirit. That starts with thinking about what you're eating versus just mindlessly eating.

- **Pause before eating.**

  Ask yourself, *Where did this food in front of me come from? How did it grow? Who harvested it?* Bringing even this little bit of check-in brings us into the moment, so we can transform this moment into one of mindfulness, gratitude, and nourishment. It's not about being perfect or restrictive but about bringing more awareness and intention to how we fuel our body, mind, and spirit.

- **Notice how different foods make you feel.**

  Are you energized or depleted, focused or foggy, soothed or inflamed?

- **Step away from your desk and screens for meals.**

Even if just for a few minutes, you have to force yourself to take that time. Thirty minutes for lunch to sit down and just eat and not do anything else is priceless.

Moving at Work

Our bodies are built to move. Yet in today's sedentary work culture, we spend hours on end sitting still, staring at screens. This takes a huge toll over time.

The solution is simple but not always easy: prioritize regular physical activity. It doesn't matter what that activity is. Find movement you enjoy and do it consistently, ideally for at least thirty minutes most days. For me, it's running. But if running isn't your thing, dancing, gardening, swimming, yoga, biking, weight training, and playing with your kids and your pup are all great options. The key is to choose activities you genuinely enjoy so you'll stick with them. Focus on how good it feels to get your blood pumping, your muscles working, and your lungs breathing deeply.

It's also vital to weave more movement into your workday. A five-day workweek is very conducive to losing track of what our bodies are doing and how they're feeling. Just taking five minutes to breathe before the next call can be transformative. In Shelby's workplace, a team she supports instituted a policy by which you can be five minutes late for each call, so there are five minutes during which you can get in touch with your body and not just have back-to-back-to-back-to-back meetings.

THE FOLLOWING ARE OTHER EASY WAYS TO SNEAK IN MORE MOVEMENT:

- Set a timer to get up and stretch every hour.
- Take phone calls or meetings while walking.
- Bike or walk partway to work.
- Do chair yoga or desk exercises.
- Use a standing desk or stability ball chair.
- Take the stairs instead of the elevator.

It helps to think of movement as a way not of stepping away from our work but stepping into it. We can make physical activity a productive pause, a chance to reconnect with ourselves and what matters most. We can approach movement not as one more task to rush through but as an act of self-care, a way to get out of our heads and into our bodies, releasing stress and coming home to ourselves. By exercising like a kid again, we move not to punish our bodies but to celebrate them.

Our bodies are ancient. Our bodies are wise. Yet we've become disconnected. We can remain connected with our spirits by connecting with our bodies. This is a superpower that we have.

Don't Skimp on Sleep

Arianna Huffington, cofounder of the *Huffington Post*, was a self-described "sleep evangelist" who learned the hard way about the importance of listening to her body. In 2007 she collapsed from exhaustion and burnout, hitting her head on her desk and breaking her cheekbone. This painful wake-up call forced her to reevaluate her priorities and make self-care a nonnegotiable part of her life.

As she recounted in her book *The Sleep Revolution*, Huffington realized that her relentless pursuit of success had come at a steep cost to her health and well-being.

"I had to literally hit my head against the desk to understand the importance of sleep," she wrote.[22]

This experience inspired her to become a vocal advocate for the power of sleep and the dangers of burnout culture, urging others to prioritize rest and renewal in their own lives.

Sleep is essential for every aspect of health—physical, mental, emotional, and spiritual. Most adults need seven to nine hours per night for optimal functioning. Yet in our fast-paced modern world, sacrificing sleep to work longer hours is often seen as a badge of honor. Between the pressure to be "always on" and the constant stimulation of screens, caffeine, sugar, and other substances, it's no wonder so many of us are chronically tired.

Sleep deprivation not only tanks productivity but also wreaks havoc on every system of the body. The person who doesn't sleep develops high blood pressure and worse. Sleep is needed for the body to rejuvenate itself and come back for another day.

So how can we reclaim rest in a sleep-deprived world? Start by setting and protecting nonnegotiable sleep hours. Count backward from when you need to wake up. If you're aiming for seven hours and need to be up at 6:00 a.m., that means lights out by 11:00 p.m. at the latest.

Of course, falling asleep and staying asleep can be challenging if you're wired from work stress and screens. Getting things off your mind

---

22 Arianna Huffington, *The Sleep Revolution: Transforming Your Life, One Night at a Time* (Harmony Books, 2017), 3.

before sleeping is key but not always possible. I've often found myself getting up to solve work-related problems in the middle of the night.

I think we all know to put our phone in a different room at night so we cannot reach for it. This takes discipline. We are retraining our brains to get over the addictive nature of the tech. But getting our lives back and keeping our spirits intact requires discipline from us as individuals because it is not going to come from the corporation.

A consistent wind-down routine before bed can help us separate from work-related stress. For example, using an old-fashioned note pad and pen to get any work-related open topics down on paper and off your mind before sleeping as a way to "park" work until the next day.

IN ADDITION TO READING SOMETHING RELAXING, OTHER HELPFUL PRESLEEP RITUALS INCLUDE THE FOLLOWING:

- Turning off screens at least an hour before bed
- Taking a warm bath
- Practicing gentle bedtime yoga or stretching
- Meditating or doing a "body scan" to release tension
- Journaling to offload worries and stress
- Diffusing lavender or other calming essential oils
- Sipping chamomile or passionflower tea

While it may feel unproductive in the moment, protecting your sleep is one of the best investments you can make in your overall well-being and performance. When you give your body and mind the gift of deep rest, you set yourself up to show up with more clarity, creativity, and resilience during your waking hours.

Stressing over Stress

I once worked with a man who told me, "I don't feel stressed ever. I can be put in really challenging situations, and I'll just go after it." He was one of those people who are so common in the corporation, who will power through no matter what.

Then one day he was sitting at his computer, having trouble resolving a critical bug in the code, and all of a sudden, he doubled over. He had to go to the emergency room. We all thought maybe he had a terrible, sudden stomach flu or had eaten something bad. But days later, after he returned to the office, he said, "That was my body telling me that I couldn't take the stress anymore."

He was so disconnected from his body that he hadn't even realized stress had been building up inside of him for so long. This was his body trying to say, "Hello! Something has to change here!"

And it does need to change. Researcher and physician Hans Selye, who founded stress theory, was one of the first to promote the idea that stress leads to physical disease. He noted that "every stress leaves an indelible scar, and the organism pays for its survival after a stressful situation by becoming a little older."[23] He turned out to be right. Chronic stress weakens the immune system, impairs digestion, disrupts sleep, and contributes to anxiety, depression, diabetes, heart disease, and other illnesses.[24]

I am also someone who has ignored my body's signals and tried to power through. If you had asked me early in my career if I felt stress, I would have also said no. Or even more accurately, I would have said that I thrived on stress. It made me work harder and better. It is definitely a balance, and I think this attitude is starting to change with

---

23 Hans Selye, *The Stress of Life*, second edition (New York: McGraw-Hill, 1976).

24 "Stress Effects on the Body," American Psychological Association, accessed March 28, 2024, https://www.apa.org/topics/stress/body.

the next generations, to move away from perpetuating a "productivity at all costs" culture where relaxation is a revolutionary act. Avoiding too much stress is essential for maintaining your spirit, and you only know if the stress is too much by listening to your body's signals.

While we can't always control the external stressors we face, we can learn to manage our inner responses. It helps me to make time to connect with a sense of inner peace and presence with an awareness practice, but it's different for everyone. For some, like Shelby, a meditation practice can help. For others, it could be mindful movement such as yoga. Even simple activities such as walking in nature, taking a relaxing bath, or savoring a cup of tea can become a mindfulness practice when approached with presence and intention.

I think this attitude is starting to change with the next generations, to move away from perpetuating a "productivity at all costs" culture where relaxation is a revolutionary act. Avoiding too much stress is essential for maintaining your spirit, and you only know if the stress is too much by listening to your body's signals.

The key is to prioritize these "stress breaks" before you reach the breaking point. To do this, you need to keep checking in with your body. Is something amiss? Time to pause.

For example, a coworker had come to understand that one of the things that caused her the greatest stress was being interrupted. It made her feel "not just talked over but walked over."

She controls her stress by controlling her response to these interruptions by saying to herself, "This is an opportunity for me to grow. It's crucial to be seen and heard in a corporation, and so I need to stand up for myself." When she's interrupted, she responds immediately and firmly, "Please let me finish my point," or "I was talking. Can we hold that thought for a moment?"

Numbing the Body

A recent study by the American Bar Association found that 21 percent of lawyers and others in the legal profession struggled with alcohol abuse.[25] And 15 percent of healthcare professionals developed a substance abuse at some time in their careers, almost 5 percent higher than the general population.[26] This is all to say when our workplaces are stressful, many of us turn to drugs and alcohol.

I don't judge people who use substances as a way of dealing with stress. The world we're living in is hard, and coping isn't always easy. The problem is that relying on any substance to manage stress only disconnects us further from our bodies and thus from our true needs. Alcohol is one of the most problematic substances because it's normalized in corporate culture.

While it's important not to judge others' choices, it's equally important to be honest with ourselves about the impact of substance use on our well-being. Using substances is the opposite of listening to your body; in many cases, it's actively silencing your body. Masking stress with substances means that the stress still exists—it's just temporarily buried.

Also, when we use substances, we often miss the chance to solve the systemic, structural problems of our workplaces that might otherwise be fixed. When we address systemic issues, we not only help ourselves but also support others, fostering a sense of unity and shared purpose. For instance, Shelby introduced breathing exercises to her team. This simple act not only helped her manage her own

---

25 Priscilla Henson, ed., "Addiction & Substance Abuse in Lawyers: Statistics to Know," American Addiction Centers, June 21, 2024, https://americanaddictioncenters.org/workforce-addiction/white-collar/lawyers.

26 Ashley Bayliss, ed., "Drug & Alcohol Addiction Treatment Centers," BetterAddictionCare.com, February 23, 2024, https://betteraddictioncare.com/addiction/substance-abuse/healthcare-professionals/.

stress but also created a supportive environment for her colleagues and promoted a healthier work culture.

It's not always easy to be honest with ourselves about the role that substances play in our lives. It's also not easy to explore alternative ways of cultivating well-being. However, finding more sustainable paths to success and fulfillment in our work and our lives will benefit our spirit in the long run.

Prioritizing Your Spirit

Prioritizing means identifying the most critical tasks and goals and focusing your time and energy on those first. Make it your priority to maintain your spirit by being in touch with your body. As is always the case, it's about being strategic and intentional with your resources rather than getting caught up in the urgency of the moment. Prioritizing your physical health is not selfish; it's imperative.

Of course, you still need to prioritize your work. You'll put in long hours; push through your lunch of coffee and whatever is available at that moment, whether it is nutritious or not; and stay up much too late. But when you keep in mind the damage that's done during this time, remember Shelby at her silent ten-day retreat: you don't have to take ten days, but take ten minutes to start right here, right now, by tuning in to your body's wisdom and giving yourself permission to put your well-being first.

Our body has innate wisdom and healing power that is always available to us if we are willing to pay attention. The more we practice listening to and honoring our body's messages, the more we strengthen the mind-body connection. In a world that constantly demands more of us, this is a radical act of self-love and self-preservation. And it just might be the key to saving your spirit.

ROADBLOCK:

Not being in touch with your physical body

CORE LESSONS CHAPTER SIX: LISTENING TO YOUR BODY

1. **Recognize the disconnect between your body and your work.**

   In the modern workplace, we often ignore our bodies' needs, sitting for hours in front of screens, skipping meals, sacrificing sleep, and numbing ourselves with caffeine and other substances in the name of productivity. This disconnection from our bodies leads to physical and spiritual suffering.

2. **Prioritize listening to your body, even when it's challenging.**

   The solution is to learn to listen to our bodies again, even though it can be difficult in a workplace culture that glorifies pushing yourself to the limit. It takes willpower and intention to prioritize our physical well-being. Check out HeartMath.org and the heartmath technique to help manage the mind and emotions in the moment.

3. **Understand and meet your body's four core needs.**

   Our bodies have four core needs: nutrition, movement, rest, and relaxation. Pay attention to what you eat, make time for regular physical activity, set nonnegotiable sleep hours, and find ways to manage stress through practices such as meditation, running, yoga, or walking your pup.

4. **Be mindful of the impact of substance use on your well-being.**

   Many people turn to substances such as alcohol or prescription drugs to cope with work-related stress, but this only disconnects us further from our bodies and our true needs. Be honest with yourself about the impact of substance use and explore healthier coping mechanisms.

5. **Embrace small acts of self-care to strengthen the mind-body connection.**

   Prioritizing our physical health is not selfish; it's imperative. Even small acts of self-care, such as taking a few deep breaths or savoring a cup of tea or coffee, can help us tune into our body's wisdom and strengthen the mind-body connection.

6. **Ask yourself the following questions:**

- What is your body telling you right now? Are you tired, tense, energized, relaxed?
- How do you typically respond to your body's needs and messages? Do you usually ignore them or honor them?
- How does your workplace culture support or hinder self-care and stress management? What is one small way you could advocate for positive change?
- Recall a time when you listened to and honored your body's wisdom. What was the situation, and how did you feel afterward?
- What is one commitment you want to make to yourself and your body going forward?

CHAPTER SEVEN

RECOGNIZING AND APPRECIATING ACHIEVEMENTS

Celebrating your own, your team's, and your peers' achievements to keep spirits strong

I try to bring joy to others. I genuinely like the people I work with and make a point as a team lead to find ways to bring the team together to build deep personal connections. Not forced corporate fun, mind you, but truly caring about each other's lives.

—MANISHA ARORA, CORPORATE SPIRIT-KEEPER AND SENIOR DIRECTOR, SERVICENOW

Recognition matters. The lack of recognition for achievements can dampen morale and spirit. When we deny this aspect of our humanity, we dampen our own spirits. When our managers fail to acknowledge and celebrate their team members' input and successes, it leads to feelings of underappreciation, demotivation, and even burnout. And when whole corporate cultures are built around the idea that recognition isn't important, we see across-the-board loss of spirit.

This hurts not just employees but also the corporation itself. In an environment where recognition is scarce, employees feel like their hard work goes unnoticed. They can become disengaged. This, in turn, can result in lower productivity and higher turnover rates and lead to a general decline in the company's overall performance.

Moreover, when managers themselves lack the desire or capacity to recognize their team's achievements, it can create a ripple effect throughout the organization. Employees who don't feel appreciated may be less likely to celebrate their peers' successes, fostering a culture of indifference and competition rather than collaboration and support.

To combat this, it is crucial for individuals, managers, and peers to find ways to recognize and appreciate their and their team's achievements, even when the larger organization fails to do so.

When achievements at work go unrecognized, it can feel discouraging and demotivating. However, there are constructive ways to handle this situation and ensure contributions are acknowledged.

The Need to Celebrate

Growing up, my family didn't have much in the way of celebrations or rituals. My parents were divorced, and I lived with my mother, who worked many jobs through the years to support us. This meant that the joy and excitement that typically come with special occasions were often absent or, worse, replaced by added stress.

In my own family, I have established rituals and celebrate milestones. One particularly meaningful ritual I started was a monthly game night for my extended family, including my in-laws who are in their nineties. Feeling that time was precious, I wanted to create lasting memories with the people I loved. Even though it was a simple gesture, those game nights brought us closer together and gave us a reason to celebrate each other's company.

In my professional life, I've tried to bring that sense of celebration and ritual to my work. I make a point of recognizing my colleagues' achievements, whether it's through a heartfelt email, a small gift, flowers, or a public acknowledgment of a job well done. I've found that by celebrating others' successes, I bring joy not only to their lives but also to my own, keeping all our spirits intact.

Through these experiences, I've learned that celebrations and rituals don't have to be grand or expensive. It's about taking the time to acknowledge the people and moments that matter most. This is the kind of celebration we need at work. I also learned that just as my mother's financial struggles made it difficult for us to celebrate milestones and create meaningful rituals, a manager's leadership style can greatly impact how our achievements are recognized in the workplace. Understanding the different types of managers and their approaches to recognition is crucial for knowing how to best approach your specific situation in your workplace.

Kinds of Managers

In the corporate world, you'll encounter a variety of managers, each with their unique leadership style. Recognizing these different types of managers is crucial for understanding how much or how little you need to bring to the table to celebrate your and your peers' achievements effectively. These are the three management styles to consider when it comes to celebrating achievements.

KINDS OF MANAGERS

- **Reluctant Leaders**

  These are managers who never aspired to manage others but found themselves in a leadership role. These managers may lack the passion or skills to develop and recognize their team members effectively. You have to take a step back and give these folks a break. It doesn't help to try to blame or shame them. If you find yourself working under a reluctant leader, you can take the initiative to communicate the appreciation of your peers' achievements. Seek feedback from other sources, such as colleagues or mentors, and don't hesitate to self-advocate during performance reviews.

- **Glory Seekers**

  These are managers who crave the spotlight and take credit for their team's successes. Working with a glory seeker can be challenging, as they rarely acknowledge or celebrate individual or team achievements beyond their own. In this situation, you also have to focus on building strong relationships with your peers and other leaders within the organization. Celebrate your colleagues' successes, and create a culture of mutual appreciation within your team. By fostering a supportive environment, you can keep spirits high, despite a disappointing lack of response from above.

- **Dream Managers**

  These are managers who genuinely appreciate and acknowledge their team members' accomplishments and care about their team members' growth. If you're lucky enough to work with a manager like this, embrace the opportunity to learn and grow under their leadership. Take note of how they celebrate achievements and strive to emulate their approach when recognizing your peers' successes. Share your accomplishments with your manager and express gratitude for their support and guidance, celebrating them in return.

Trusting Your Inner Compass

In my decades of navigating the corporate world, I've learned that one of the most crucial skills is knowing your worth and trusting in the value you bring to your work. It's easy to get caught up in seeking external validation, waiting for that pat on the back or glowing performance review. But the truth is, you might not always get the recognition you deserve, especially if you have a reluctant or glory-seeking manager or work in an organization without a culture of celebration.

I've worked with people who are entirely dependent on external validation, and this is a precarious situation to be in, constantly relying on others to affirm their worth. In contrast, I've found that Spirit-Keepers almost always have a strong sense of self and trust in their abilities.

This doesn't mean you should be blind to feedback or ignore constructive criticism. Everyone needs input and guidance to grow and improve. However, it's essential to develop an internal compass that guides you and a deep understanding of your strengths, weaknesses, and the value you contribute.

Start by setting your standards of excellence. When you pour your heart and soul into a project, when you know you've given it your all, take a moment to acknowledge and celebrate that effort, regardless of the external response. Recognize that your dedication and hard work have inherent value, even if others don't always see it. A colleague shared this with me:

> "First and foremost, I answer to myself. Since I am most familiar with my successes and failures, I trust my judgment on whether or not I have been effective. I gain confidence with hits and learn from misses. While I do enjoy recognition, I have no expectations in terms of third-party (manager or otherwise) appreciation and do not need that to move forward."

Here are some standards I hold myself to. When I meet these, I pat myself on the back and move on.

1. Work as hard as I can.
2. Stay committed to my goals.
3. Maintain a positive attitude throughout the process.
4. Consistently find ways to improve my skills.
5. Complete my tasks with integrity.
6. Remain focused and avoid distractions.
7. Take initiative to solve problems.
8. Effectively manage my time and resources.
9. Collaborate well with my team members and give credit to others continuously.
10. Learn from mistakes and adapt accordingly.

Cultivating this self-awareness and self-appreciation is a continuous process. It requires you to be honest with yourself, to regularly assess your performance, and to trust in your capabilities. By doing so you build resilience and confidence, which are essential for navigating the challenges and triumphs of your career.

Being Your Own Best Advocate

While cultivating a strong sense of self-worth and trusting in your abilities is essential, it's not enough to keep your spirit intact. As human beings, we crave external validation and recognition for our hard work and achievements. Moreover, operating under the radar and not being noticed for our contributions can be detrimental to our career. That's why it's crucial to take proactive steps to advocate for yourself and ensure that your accomplishments are visible and celebrated.

HERE ARE WAYS TO ADVOCATE FOR YOURSELF:

- **Don't shy away from promoting your work.**

  Example: In your regular one-on-ones with your manager, discuss your recent project success, your team leadership and collaboration, and its impact on the company.

- **Keep a detailed record of your accomplishments.**

  Example: Create a "success journal" to track your weekly or monthly achievements, such as completing your projects ahead of schedule, helping team members meet their goals, and receiving praise from colleagues. It'll come in handy when it's time for your performance review.

- **Actively seek input from a variety of sources.**

  Example: Ask colleagues from other departments for their honest feedback on your presentation skills after a company-wide meeting. Appreciate the feedback and look at ways you can do better.

- **Work with your manager to establish clear, measurable goals.**

  Example: If it is not common in your organization, work with your manager to set clear, measurable goals and discuss your progress regularly to keep your achievements front and center.

- **Constantly seek external opportunities.**

  Example: Talk to recruiters and industry peers to validate and reassess your worth.

- **Seek external recognition for you and your team.**

  Example: Seek out and pursue industry awards. When you win, tell the world through company emails, newsletters, small prizes, or public celebrations.

Being your own best advocate is an ongoing process that requires continuous effort and attention, but the reward of a constantly reinvigorated spirit is worth the trouble.

Spreading a Culture of Mutual Appreciation

Knowing how to celebrate the achievements of others isn't simple. Fostering a culture of mutual appreciation requires consistent effort and a variety of approaches.

Dr. Gary Chapman, the *New York Times* best-selling author of *The 5 Love Languages*, wrote a sequel called *The 5 Languages of Appreciation in the Workplace*. In that book he tailored his ideas of love languages to the context of professional relationships and team dynamics.

Here are his ways to show appreciation in the workplace:[27]

- **Words of Affirmation**

Words of affirmation involve expressing appreciation through spoken or written words to affirm someone else's work and value. An example of this is sending handwritten notes—which is entirely unheard of in our digital world, but a gesture that stands out amidst the texts and chats. Take the time to write a personalized note acknowledging a colleague's contribution, whether they stayed late to help meet a deadline or went above and beyond on a project. It's a simple gesture that can make a big impact.

Another way to affirm with words is with a public shoutout. You can use team meetings or company communication channels to highlight a coworker's success. It encourages others to do the same. The best way to do this may just be saying, "Thank you." One 2023 study found that a genuine "thank you" created a 69 percent increase in

27 Gary Chapman and Paul White, *The 5 Languages of Appreciation in the Workplace: Empowering Organizations by Encouraging People* (Chicago: Northfield Publishing, 2019).

the likelihood of employees putting in extra effort in the future.[28]

- **Quality Time**

Giving someone your undivided attention can help them feel valued. This can be as simple as spending time in a one-on-one meeting for a virtual coffee break.

- **Acts of Service**

Helping a colleague, especially when they are under pressure, will lighten their load and boost their spirits.

- **Tangible Gifts**

Giving unexpected small gifts that are meaningful to colleagues is always appreciated.

Whatever kind of language you use to express appreciation, finding joy in others' achievements will increase your spirit. I've found that one of the most powerful ways to boost morale, productivity, and overall job satisfaction is by fostering a culture of peer recognition and mutual appreciation. When you actively celebrate the accomplishments of your colleagues, it not only makes them feel valued but also establishes a positive workplace dynamic where everyone feels more connected and supported. And the more Spirit-Keepers around us, the more likely we are to hold on to our spirits.

It's crucial to remember that celebrating others' successes doesn't diminish your achievements. It can even enhance your spirit and create a more supportive work environment for everyone.

---

28 Claire Hastwell, "Creating a Culture of Recognition," Insights, March 2, 2023, https://www.greatplacetowork.com/resources/blog/creating-a-culture-of-recognition.

When You're the Manager

As a manager, one of your most important responsibilities is to recognize and celebrate the achievements of your team members. By actively supporting and advocating for your colleagues, you can foster a positive and productive work environment where everyone feels valued and appreciated—a team that others in the organization will want to be a part of. You don't have to be a formal manager to do this. In my last corporate role, I did not manage anyone directly. And yet, since I still needed to pull in others on projects, I still celebrated their achievements as a manager would by doing the following:

- **Giving direct and regular feedback**

  I make it a point to provide direct and frequent feedback to virtual team members. When working across the organization, I told one of my partners, "I'm the luckiest person in the world that I get to work with you." I do this because it is true and I think it is important to express this and because regular, positive feedback is crucial for building confidence, motivation, and keeping everyone's spirit intact.

- **Passing on accolades to team members**

  When the accolades start coming in, it's important to always share them with the team. One person I interviewed for this book explained, "In a well-functioning team, a team member's growth energizes others. It's a joy to have high-achieving peers because they inspire and, in many cases, enable others around them to do better. The virtuous cycle lifts everyone up."

- **Advocating for recognition**

  There are so many ways you can advocate for your team members. Financial rewards are always appreciated, including advocating for raises, bonuses, and promotions. Sometimes, it's just taking the time and sticking your neck out for the small things that seem to matter most. Recognition within the team is important to foster. A manager I interviewed for this book suggested asking a high achiever to share their best practices with their peers and "even my managers, so we can all learn to replicate their successes where possible while elevating the high performers' visibility and credibility within the organization."

Rethink the manager role so that celebrating others is not just a nice thing to do; it's a fundamental part of creating a strong, supportive, and successful team.

Celebrating "Followership"

As teams form and dissolve, you may run a project one month and contribute the next. This fluidity underscores the importance of recognizing all kinds of achievements, even tasks and people who may seem peripheral to a project. Robert Kelley, a distinguished professor at Carnegie Mellon University, calls these people "followers." He identifies the following five styles of followership, all necessary and worthy of celebrating:

1. **Sheep:** People who are wholly passive. For example, in a financial services company, Emma diligently follows instructions without seeking to understand the bigger picture. Her

reliability ensures data integrity, which is crucial for accurate financial reporting.

2. **Yes-People:** People who enthusiastically do what the boss wants but never think for themselves. For example, Alex implements every campaign idea from the manager with enthusiasm. His proactive attitude helps maintain the team's momentum and ensures all campaigns are executed on schedule.
3. **Alienated Followers:** People who think for themselves but mainly critique the organization. For example, James frequently points out flaws in the system but also proposes innovative solutions. His constructive criticism and proactive suggestions drive significant improvements in the company's software products.
4. **Pragmatists:** People who get on board with things but rarely initiate changes. For example, Sarah ensures deadlines are met without initiating new ideas. Her focus on maintaining project stability ensures that all phases of the construction proceed smoothly and on time.
5. **Stars:** People who think for themselves, have positivity and energy, and offer constructive criticism. For example, Mia inspires her colleagues with her work ethic and provides constructive feedback. Her leadership fosters team growth and motivates everyone to achieve higher performance standards.[29]

You may think that only the stars deserve celebration, but all of these followers, regardless of their style, contribute to the overall success

29 "How to Be a Good Follower: First, Realise That It Matters," *Economist*, May 16, 2024. https://www.economist.com/business/2024/05/16/how-to-be-a-good-follower.

of a team and should be noted. If you're a leader or a teammate, be sure to notice and celebrate the nonstars too. And if you're a follower, be aware of what type of follower you are, and celebrate yourself accordingly. Everyone does their part, and it takes a team to succeed.

ROADBLOCK:

Not putting in the time and effort to celebrate yourself or others at work

---

CORE LESSONS CHAPTER SEVEN: CELEBRATING ACHIEVEMENTS

1. **Recognize that the need for celebration and recognition is a fundamental human need.**

   Don't dismiss or downplay this for yourself or others.

2. **Be aware of the type of manager you're working with (reluctant leader, glory seeker, dream manager).**

   Adapt your approach to get recognized accordingly.

3. **Cultivate a strong internal sense of self-worth.**

   Trust your abilities and don't rely solely on external validation.

4. **Be your own best advocate.**

   Document your achievements, seek feedback, set goals with your manager, and explore external options if needed.

5. **Spread a culture of mutual appreciation among peers.**

   Use handwritten notes, public shout-outs, celebration boards, peer-nominated awards, and small gifts.

6. **Find genuine joy in celebrating the achievements of others.**

   It enhances your own spirit and work environment.

7. **As a manager, give overt and regular positive feedback to boost confidence and motivation in your team.**

   Share credit and spotlight team members' contributions, don't hoard accolades, and don't let jealousy or competitiveness hinder their growth.

8. **Ask yourself the following questions:**

- When was the last time you celebrated a colleague's success? How did this act of recognition impact your relationship and the overall team dynamic?
- Which of the languages of appreciation in the workplace resonates most with you? How can you use this insight to better appreciate your colleagues?
- Reflect on a time when you received meaningful recognition at work. What made this recognition particularly impactful? How can you apply these insights when recognizing others?

CHAPTER EIGHT

INTEGRATE YOUR LIFE AND WORK

Navigating the fluidity between work and personal life

At the still point of the turning world.

—T. S. ELIOT, "BURNT NORTON," 1935

About two decades ago, while working in a global role at a major international corporation, I was starting to experience ways in which work didn't have to be tied to a physical office. This insight into how we might approach work led me to create an internal guide called "Managing in the Virtual Workplace." Nobody was talking about remote or flexible work. At that time it wasn't even a thing. Despite the lack of precedent, I was convinced this was the direction we should be heading.

However, my corporation's leadership at that time was not supportive of the idea of a virtual workplace. I don't think many other companies were leaning into this future either. Most believed in the idea that good management came from regularly walking around the site to make time to see and speak with employees, which meant employees had to be physically at their desks. These leaders also touted the serendipitous conversations around the office "water cooler" that they believed led to innovation. But in a global world with teams spread out across countries and borders, there is no physical "water cooler."

Fast-forward to today and the world of work has evolved tremendously. With the rise of technology and the onset of the COVID-19 pandemic, flexible, remote work has become the norm for many. No longer is work defined by a physical place. And yet remote work hasn't always turned out to be the panacea I had originally envisioned. Many of us find that we're more constantly connected and overwhelmed by work than ever.

With the boundaries between work and life blurred, we can struggle to find balance. For many, we're always on, always available. The burden of being tethered to the office has been replaced with the challenge of being tethered to our devices. Instead of remote work being a solution to spirit loss, it has made work all-consuming, leading to unprecedented levels of stress and burnout. Our phones and devices have become an addiction, negatively impacting our spirits. As someone who's long seen and championed the benefits of flexible work, I know it doesn't have to be this way.

To combat the spirit-draining effects of the blurring of work boundaries and digital intrusion, we must reframe our understanding of how work and life intersect. For years, people talked about a work-life balance. But that terminology has gone by the wayside, as many found it not helpful and impossible to achieve. The problem is that work-life balance implies that there is an ideal combination—maybe fifty-fifty. In fact, sometimes, work demands 100 percent of us, and sometimes, our outside commitments demand 100 percent.

This is why we need instead to accept fluidity into our lives by intentionally integrating our professional and personal lives. To do this, we must find a place of peace amid chaos. This becomes our touchpoint. T. S. Eliot called this "the still point of the turning world." By setting firm boundaries, priorities, and goals, we've created a still point on which our world can turn. With this at the center of our mindset, we can do our work, hold on to our lives outside work, and protect our spirits from burnout.

The Modern Workplace

We all know that colleague who takes great pride in their nonstop work. They start their workday early and work into the night and on weekends. They talk about their grueling schedule and long hours.

This is neither healthy nor sustainable. These people are caught on a hamster wheel of their own making, driven by ambition and external validation. But working this way isn't normal, and it shouldn't be celebrated. Even if your workplace's culture rewards this 24/7 mentality, you don't have to buy into the idea that this is what success looks like, no matter the personal cost.

As a society, we're reaching a breaking point. There are human costs of this 24/7 work. A recent study by the World Health Organization found that working fifty-five hours or more per week is associated with a 35 percent higher risk of stroke and a 17 percent higher risk of dying from heart disease compared with working thirty-five to forty hours a week.[30] We need a fundamental shift in how we approach

---

30 "Long Working Hours Increasing Deaths from Heart Disease and Stroke: WHO, ILO," World Health Organization, May 17, 2021, https://www.who.int/news/item/17-05-2021-long-working-hours-increasing-deaths-from-heart-disease-and-stroke-who-ilo.

work—not just for our own well-being but also for the health of our families and communities.

So how do we break free from this cycle? How can we redefine success in a way that honors our spirits? The answer is both straightforward and not always easy: we must be intentional in integrating work and life. This requires effort at three levels:

- Individual
- Leadership
- Organization-wide

By being intentional at every level, we can create a profound shift in how we live and work. It begins with what we can control ourselves at the individual level.

Setting Boundaries

Growing up, my mom struggled mightily to integrate work and life. As a single mom, she worked multiple jobs trying to make ends meet. She didn't have a college degree, so her work options were limited. She had to be away from home a lot. While I admired her incredible work ethic and determination, I also felt the void of her absence.

When my husband and I discussed having children, we committed to being fully present as parents, to not being absent in our child's life in the way I had experienced despite my mother's heroic efforts. We would work hard to always be there for our daughter's milestones and activities. To us, this meant taking time off work to volunteer in her classroom, attend sports events, and be present for those special school moments.

My husband exemplified his commitment from the day our daughter was born. He said, "I am not going to miss anything. I'm not going to miss any school plays. I'm not going to miss any soccer games." And he stayed true to his word throughout our daughter's childhood. His intention was clear, and his actions followed suit.

We also agreed that we wanted to be financially secure and have reliable childcare in place before we had a child. This meant that we didn't have a child until I was forty. In those days, forty was considered an older mother, but I could never have imagined having our daughter sooner without being financially ready. I know that this isn't a path that's available to everyone. And I know that many choose other equally viable paths. What is important isn't what you do but that you do it with intention, commitment, and a plan.

Still, it wasn't always easy despite having office jobs that could accommodate the flexibility we needed. I was fortunate that I was already working remotely when we had our daughter. This allowed me to work remotely out of the house and have someone come in during the weekdays to help with childcare.

It's important to recognize that working excessively for your family's benefit doesn't help if you're never actually present with them. But being present isn't just about physical proximity. It's about giving your full attention and engagement. I had a colleague who, when his child was born, took three months of paternity leave. He recognized the importance of bonding with his newborn, telling me, "I never bonded with my first child." He was determined to do things differently the second time around. I have another colleague who shared that when his daughters were younger, his work got more attention than his daughters did, until one day his wife came to him and said, "You know how the girls are always asking if Daddy is going to be home for dinner? Well, they have stopped asking." He shared that this was a turning point for him and his family to change, focus, and reinforce boundaries.

Many of us do not take advantage of the benefits we have available. For example, it's been noted that when corporations offer unlimited paid time off, most people actually end up taking fewer days away.[31] Another study found that 46 percent of workers didn't take their paid time off. When asked why, 52 percent reported that they didn't "feel the need," 49 percent worried "they might fall behind," 43 percent said they felt "badly about co-workers taking on additional work," and 19 percent reported that they thought more time off "might hurt their chances for job advancement." Only 16 percent said that their manager or supervisor discouraged them from taking the time they were entitled to.[32]

These numbers highlight the importance of making intentional choices to be present for our families. Having a plan, setting boundaries with work, communicating our priorities, and then following through with action by actually taking the time we're offered can be the difference between saving your spirit and burnout.

In August of 2024, Australia put in place the Right to Disconnect Law that allows workers to ignore calls and emails after hours. Prime Minister Anthony Albanese told the Australian Broadcasting Corporation, "For many Australians, I think they're getting frustrated that they're expected to be on their phones, their emails, all of that, twenty-four hours a day," he said. "It's a mental health issue, frankly." He added that he expects these changes to also boost productivity.[33]

---

31 Rachel Bolsu, "IMHRO: Why Unlimited Vacation Isn't a Fools Errand - Namely," Namely HR, July 30, 2024, https://namely.com/blog/why-unlimited-vacation-isnt-a-fools-errand/.

32 Emily Peck, "Americans Aren't Taking All of Their Paid Time Off from Work," Axios, March 30, 2023, https://www.axios.com/2023/03/30/americans-pto-time-off-survey.

33 Ben Westcott, "Australia Gives Workers 'Right to Disconnect,'" Time, August 26, 2024, https://time.com/7014775/australia-right-to-disconnect-law-work-calls-employers-fine/.

Managing Work Travel

Consider what travel cadence is sustainable for you and what the impact of your absence is on your loved ones. Look for ways to minimize travel when possible, such as through virtual meetings or strategic trip planning.

HERE ARE SOME WAYS TO ASK YOUR MANAGER TO ALLOW YOU TO STOP TRAVELING:

1. **Evaluate Your Current Situation:**

   Assess the impact of travel on your personal and professional life to clearly understand your needs.

2. **Prepare Your Case:**

   Gather data and examples that highlight how reducing travel will benefit both you and the company.

3. **Be Clear and Direct:**

   Clearly state your request to stop or significantly reduce travel, explaining your reasons concisely.

4. **Offer Alternatives:**

   Suggest viable alternatives such as remote work, virtual meetings, or strategically planned trips.

5. **Highlight Benefits:**

   Emphasize how reduced travel can lead to increased productivity, better work-life balance, and overall well-being.

6. **Address Concerns:**

   Be prepared to address any concerns your manager might have and offer solutions to potential issues.

7. **Show Flexibility:**

   Be open to compromise and discuss phased approaches or occasional travel if absolutely necessary.

8. **Document the Agreement:**

   Once an agreement is reached, document the terms clearly to avoid future misunderstandings.

9. **Follow Up:**

   Regularly check in with your manager to ensure the new arrangement is working well for both parties and make adjustments if needed.

Once you establish a travel schedule that works for you, try to avoid what I call "travel creep." Even when I was supposedly working mostly remotely, those weekly in-person meetings kept me on the road and in the office when many of them could have been done virtually. This wasn't good for me or my family. I'm forever grateful I was able to travel early in my career, and I cherish the lessons I learned in my travels. I am equally grateful I was able to stop later in my career, but it wasn't easy. It took intention, negotiation, and resolve.

Leaving Screens Behind

In today's always-on work culture, our devices have become an extension of ourselves. We're constantly connected, responding to emails, messages, texts, and calls at all hours. While technology has enabled remote work and flexibility, it's also led to a blurring between our professional and personal lives.

To save our spirits from burnout, we must be intentional about disconnecting from our devices and setting clear boundaries. One strategy is to set specific times to turn off our devices, such as after 8:00 p.m. or during meals. Or instead of sending emails at all hours, try writing down your thoughts in a journal or notebook. This practice can help you process your ideas without the pressure of immediate communication. One of my colleagues has made it clear that he will not be online over the weekend, and he wants his team members to know that if they are doing work over the weekend, he will not be joining them. This is a great way to lead by example.

Creating physical boundaries between work and personal life is also crucial. As one colleague who was mostly a remote worker shared with me, "I often find myself working beyond traditional hours because it's easy to get caught up in tasks when there's no physical separation between office and home. While this has its advantages in terms of productivity, it's essential to establish boundaries to prevent burnout and maintain a healthy work-life balance."

Designate a specific workspace in your home and ban work screens from areas meant for family time—even if you are the only one in the room without a screen, you are modeling for the rest of your family that they, too, can be screen-free for a few minutes. Engage in screen-free activities, such as exercise, hobbies, or spending time in nature to reduce stress and improve overall well-being.

As we all know firsthand, this is harder than it sounds because of the addictive nature of constant connection to work. As Dr. Judson Brewer, author of *The Craving Mind*, explains, "Our brain is set up with a hierarchy of behaviors based on their reward value. The behavior with the bigger reward is the one we act out."[34] We are rewarded by our constant connection through the dopamine hit we get from the "ding" of a chat message, email, or text. The dopamine hit reinforces the feeling of being needed, important, and appreciated.

Breaking the neural pathways that keep us locked into overworking takes effort and time. Dr. Brewer emphasizes that the single most important way to break our habits is through what he calls *awareness*. "To change a habit," he says, "our brains need new information so they can see that whatever the value that they had learned in the past is outdated."[35] Only by focusing intentionally on the negative results of being locked onto our devices in the present moment can we jolt our brains out of the habit of autopilot.

So next time you're with your family or friends and find yourself texting or working, cultivate awareness of the true reward. We need to literally rewire our brains by pausing and noticing how our family or friends feel and the true value of our rushed, distracted responses.

Over time, this weakened association can help us break the cycle of overworking and reclaim our time and energy. Dr. Brewer calls this "reward-based learning."[36] He points out that it can take as few as ten attempts to break the existing reward system and form a new one, so the sooner you start, the sooner you'll be able to disconnect.

When You're the Manager

As a manager, you're able to take what you believe about integrating work and life and spread it to your team. By creating a culture that

34 DrJud, "Hacking Your Brain's 'Reward System' to Change Habits," February 18, 2020, YouTube video, https://www.youtube.com/watch?v=WQ40hNdZmfQ.

35 DrJud, "Hacking."

36 DrJud.

values and prioritizes work-life integration, you'll not only help your team members save their spirits from burnout, but you'll also foster a more productive, engaged, and loyal workforce. Kathryn Guarini, former chief information officer of IBM, has worked for a lifetime in corporations. She told me,

> Most companies will take everything you are willing to give, even if and when they officially support "flexible work." It's up to you to define what you need—and stick to that. Most often, others will respect that. But you can't expect others to know what you need. So if you need to arrive or leave at a certain hour, say so. If you need to step out for any reason—to go to the gym, for a doctor's appointment, whatever—don't apologize about it. Just give fair warning and then do it. And support the same of others. Wherever possible, focus more on ***outcomes*** and ***impact*** than on hours worked or days in the office, and do this for yourself and others.

By making work-life integration a priority, you'll not only help your team save their spirits from burnout, but you'll also create a more sustainable and successful organization in the long run.

Guarini emphasizes, "Flexibility does not just mean remote/virtual/hybrid versus in person, though it includes that. It also means having an environment, culture, and leadership that recognize and support life outside of work, that acknowledge that everyone has responsibilities and interests that go beyond the confines of the job, and that to be effective employees, we need to support this." She shares the following three pieces of advice that she lives by and that she hopes to spread to everyone in her organization:

1. Set boundaries

Define what success looks like for you, including what are nonnegotiables. Put a stake in the ground and commit to sticking to that.

2. Audit your calendar

One of the best tools is to block time on your calendar for the things you want to be sure to do. Prefer to get to the gym three times a week? Put it on your calendar. Expect to be home for dinner each time? Put it on the calendar. Need time to think outside of meetings? Calendar it. Periodically check how you are spending your time. If it's misaligned with your priorities, fix it.

3. Be true to yourself

Don't let others define success for you or how you'll live your life. Stay true to yourself. Take stock regularly to see if you feel like you have a reasonable balance, and if not, make a change. Find others who inspire you. Use them as role models, but chart your own course. There is no one size fits all!

NONNEGOTIABLES: WHEN YOU MUST SAY NO.

Embrace the concept of nonnegotiables. For example, a month ahead of time, you let your team know you will be taking vacation for two days. You spent money on tickets for a flight and a concert in another city. Then the week you are planning to leave, your manager says the company has a priority deadline and asks you to not go on vacation. Do you stay, or do you go? Here, you should always say no. You are going. You paid for the tickets. You let them know a month in advance. The company will always have priorities, but they don't always have to trump yours.

The Retreat of Virtual Work for Organizations Holding on to the Past

While individual efforts to integrate work and life are crucial, lasting change often requires a shift at the organizational level. As someone who has long advocated for work-life integration, I've explored and implemented various solutions within organizations. One key area that has finally come to realization is the prevalence of virtual work.

We all benefit from hybrid and remote work. A recent study from McKinsey & Company points out that most employees point to better work-life balance as a primary benefit of hybrid and remote work, and a majority cite less fatigue and burnout.[37] Moreover, 83 percent of employees cite the ability to work more efficiently and

37 Emily Field et al., "Women in the Workplace 2023," October 5, 2023, McKinsey &Company, https://www.mckinsey.com/featured-insights/diversity-and-inclusion/women-in-the-workplace.

productively as a primary benefit of working remotely.[38] However, it's worth noting companies see this differently: only half of HR leaders say employee productivity is a primary benefit of working remotely.[39]

Many people I spoke with match this sentiment and were adamant that hybrid work is what kept them from burnout. One colleague told me, "Remote work provided the flexibility I needed to be the father that I wanted to be. If I had not been able to work remotely, my son would not have been able to go as far as he had in pursuing his passion. It would have left our family with the dreaded question of 'what if' and potentially lifelong regrets. Quite honestly, my work benefited too because I had to be ultraefficient and effective."

However, we see now these remote work policies are being walked back in some organizations. According to a recent *USA Today* article, fully remote work went from over 60 percent in 2020 to 25 percent in 2023.[40] This trend suggests that while remote work has been significantly positively embraced by employees, some companies are still resistant to fully embracing it.

If you find yourself in an organization resistant to change, focus on what you can control. As an individual, set your boundaries, communicate your needs, and seek out allies who share your values. As a leader, lead by example. At the organizational level, you can have a voice by joining employee resource groups and other grassroots initiatives that can help you advocate for work-life integration policies to drive change within your organization. These groups can provide

38 Field et al., "Women."

39 Field et al.

40 Bailey Schulz, "2023 Was the Year Return-to-Office Died. Experts Share Remote-Work Trends Expected in 2024," *USA Today*, December 26, 2023, https://www.usatoday.com/story/money/2023/12/21/remote-work-from-home-trends-2024/71991203007/.

a platform for employees to share their experiences, challenges, and ideas related to work-life integration.

For example, one colleague recently told me, "Remote work has helped me accomplish things that would have been impossible otherwise. It drove me to be a better worker, enabled me to support my wife's career and my son's passion, and helped me appreciate my employers."

Sharing these sorts of sentiments with others can help raise awareness about the importance of work-life balance and advocate for policies and practices that support it. These sorts of valuable insights and feedback to leadership teams can help shape organizational strategies and initiatives that prioritize employee well-being. By harnessing the power of employee-driven change, organizations can create a culture that truly values and supports work-life integration.

If your efforts to drive change are consistently met with resistance, it may be time to consider seeking out an organization that better aligns with your values. Remember, no job is worth sacrificing your well-being and personal life. By advocating for change at the organizational level and making intentional choices about how we work, we can create a world where work-life integration is the norm, not the exception. It won't happen overnight, but by committing to these values, we can transform our workplaces and save our spirits from burnout.

ROADBLOCK:

Not integrating your work and home life

CORE LESSONS CHAPTER EIGHT: INTEGRATING LIFE AND WORK

1. **Set clear boundaries.**

   Work and personal life need to remain separate, and you must communicate this to your employer and colleagues.

2. **Set firm priorities.**

   To be fully present for your children and partners, you must make family a priority.

3. **Be mindful.**

   Being aware of the effects of your work is key. Notice what is happening at home and work so you can correct what is out of balance.

4. **Advocate for work-life integration.**

   We'll never achieve true work-life integration until healthy policies and practices are set at the organizational level.

5. **Ask yourself the following questions:**

- Reflect on your current work schedule. Are there any habits or practices that resemble the 24/7 work mentality mentioned in the chapter? How might you adjust these to better integrate your work and personal life?
- If you're a manager, how do you currently support work-life integration for your team? What additional steps could you take to foster a culture that values this balance?
- Reflect on your "nonnegotiables" in terms of work-life integration. What are the absolute boundaries you need to set to maintain your well-being and personal commitments?

CHAPTER NINE

BE WATER

Flowing around obstacles to save your spirit

Everything can be taken from a man but one thing: the last of the human freedoms—to choose one's attitude in any given set of circumstances, to choose one's own way.

—VIKTOR FRANKL, *MAN'S SEARCH FOR MEANING*

My personal philosophy in life and work is to "be water." I adopted this from Bruce Lee, a martial arts master and actor—with a twist. Water is the most powerful compound in the universe. Water is amazing—it has strong hydrogen bonds, carries nutrients, and can flow around obstacles. Its powerful erosion capacity creates landforms such as valleys and canyons. It can absorb thermal energy, and when under high pressure, water can cut steel.

When we think of ourselves as water, we can navigate around any boulders that land in our path. Water never stops flowing. It finds its way around rocks, through crevasses, and merges with other streams, multiplying its energy and strength through collaboration.

Being Water Is a Mindset

There are three main aspects of being like water:

1. Stay focused on your goals and values.
2. Don't take obstacles personally.
3. Find adaptable ways to keep moving forward.

Unfortunately, the corporate world is full of boulders that you need to flow around. A boulder is any workplace challenge or difficult person that can wear you down and drain your spirit. In chapter 4 we talked about standing up against injustice and not backing down. That still holds. Some fights are worth the fight. But you need to know how to choose your battles. Most obstacles in the corporation aren't about injustice; they're just annoying. These obstacles come in many forms, but some of the most common boulders that are best navigated around rather than confronted head-on are as follows:

- Constant changes to projects and priorities
- Managers and colleagues who are only out for their next promotion
- Feedback from managers who are not skilled in giving feedback
- Being underresourced and overworked
- Facing repeated rejections or "noes" in your career journey

These obstacles can seem daunting, even insurmountable at times. And they can drain your spirit in a very real, constant way.

But remember, you are water. As a Spirit-Keeper, you have the power to flow around these obstacles, to keep moving forward and finding new paths. And as more people join your cause, your stream of influence will grow into a mighty river, carving new paths through the corporate landscape.

Dealing with Continuous Change

A colleague shared a story that illustrates the problem of continuous change in the corporate world. He was flying back from Asia on a Friday night after a demanding work trip. Just as he was touched down back in the United States, he received an urgent call. He needed to deliver a project by Monday. This unexpected directive meant he had to spend his entire weekend working, rearranging his plans, and pushing himself and his team to meet the new deadline. On Monday morning, after he had sent off the completed project, he got another call. The project had been canceled. All that work, all that sacrifice, all that time away from his family had been for nothing.

This is the reality of continuous change in the corporate world, and most of the time, these changes are out of our control. This is the nature of business, and it happens for any number of reasons—it could be innovation, cost cutting, customer requirements, or leadership decisions. And these changes impact you and your team. For example, your beloved project gets canceled. The initiative you worked on night and day for the last month gets shelved. The urgent deliverable you were asked to create over the only weekend after you had not been home in a month gets cut from the list. Or your project survives, but there are continuous, last-minute changes up to and even beyond the launch of your project.

Remaining calm through change is hard. But once you know that this is the rhythm of the business and that it's not personal but just the world you live in, you can handle it differently. When you've adopted the philosophy that you're water, cancelations or delays don't stop you from flowing. You just keep moving to the next effort because you understand this is how innovation evolves. Your effort is water, constantly changing, and the people executing it have to know they are also water.

When "No" Is Your Boulder

Early in my career, our sales team used a customer relationship management (CRM) platform to track their sales performance. Unfortunately, it was buggy and very hard to use. Around that same time, Salesforce came out with a CRM system that was amazing compared with what we were using. One sales manager, Cody, wanted us all to make the switch from the buggy CRM system to Salesforce. Cody did all the right things through all the right channels, but he got no traction. There was a rumor that the CRM decision-maker who chose the current CRM system was very close friends with the CEO of the CRM company itself, and their personal relationship was standing in the way of the switch.

Most people would have given up. But Cody started bringing the Salesforce software into the company in an informal, casual way. It didn't matter that those at the top were resistant to change. He just kept finding new paths to expose more people to Salesforce. Every time he did, the sales team fell in love with it. They would say, "This is so much better. It's amazing. It's incredible. Why aren't we using it?"

He would tell them, "We can't. We've been told we have to use our current system."

This is how I found out about the issue. Cody showed me the software and explained the problem with adopting it. I told him, "Don't stop. Keep doing what you're doing. You need to be water. You need to go to every organization and keep going around all the mandates to use our current CRM. Those mandates are just boulders in your way. You can go around them, and eventually, you'll wear them down."

Cody told me that later the Salesforce software caught on across the company despite the mandates to use the lower-quality CRM solution.

Cody told me later that he loved how I explained his methods as my "be water" philosophy. He said he used the method and the mindset for the rest of his career.

Cody stayed focused on what he knew was right, on what was best for the company and the sales team, even when there were obstacles in his way. Being water meant that he got things done not by confrontation but also through a persistent and adaptive approach. He found a way to flow around the obstacles and stay focused on his goal. He adapted to the corporate landscape, introducing a better solution without directly challenging the status quo. This adaptable, resilient approach is the essence of being water, and it's key to keeping your spirit intact.

I have another colleague, Steve Emerson, who is a Director of Outbound Product Management for ServiceNow and who embodies the "be water" philosophy. Before joining ServiceNow, Steve worked in corporate IT for over twenty years. He loved the ServiceNow product suite and the ServiceNow company and culture so much that he set his sights on becoming a ServiceNow solution consultant. The only problem? He had no presales experience.

Every time he applied for solution consulting roles, despite his two decades in IT, he was told no because of his lack of presales experience. He didn't let that no stop him. He took each "no" as "not now" and created a plan to ensure he landed the role he aspired to. He studied the craft of presales by interviewing successful people in his network, reading, and watching videos. He applied these skills, and within a year, he had achieved his goal of landing a presales role at ServiceNow and is now a very successful Director of Outbound Product Management for ServiceNow.

This story is a perfect example of being water. He didn't let the no stand in the way of his dreams. He found a way to navigate around the rocks to get to his goal. He built relationships, he upskilled himself, and he persevered.

In the corporate world, we face a lot of noes, such as the following:

- No, you don't have the right experience for this role.
- No, we can't allocate resources to your project.
- No, that initiative isn't a priority this quarter.
- No, you're not ready for a promotion yet.
- No, we don't have budget for that training program.
- No, your idea doesn't align with our current strategy.
- No, we won't be implementing your suggestion.
- No, you can't work flexibly outside the office.
- No, that's not part of your job description.
- No, we've always done it this way.

We have to be creative, persistent, and adaptable. We have to build relationships, gain skills, and find alternate routes. We have to keep our eyes on our goals and not let the naysayers divert us. Because the thing about water is that it never stops. It keeps flowing, keeps moving, keeps finding its way.

Finding Growth by Being Water

Growth is not a given. Seeking it out will come from you. Instead of losing hope, ask yourself, "Is this where I want to stay?" Can you find growth in a lateral move or a new organization? Can you be the water and make the change happen, taking control of your future?

Throughout my career I have often been asked why I stayed at Hewlett-Packard for so long. I always replied, "Because I got to work with and learn from incredibly talented people every single day."

Of course, some were also focused on their next promotion at the expense of the team, but I had developed a sense of who was there to help the team and do the work and who I had to flow around as swiftly and silently as possible. I developed an attitude that my growth and learning came from the people I was working with every day, and the others, I could flow around.

Movement was the point, the method, and the reason for my surviving with my spirit intact.

After being in a role for three or four years, when I was ready to find new growth, I would seek out a new role within HP. This wasn't necessarily an upward change but a change to keep learning and growing. By being water and adaptively seeking out new opportunities for growth and development, I was able to keep moving forward in my career, even when the path ahead wasn't always a straight line. It's key that you don't let your ambition turn you into a boulder. Keep moving, keep growing, and keep seeking out new opportunities to contribute and learn.

Feedback: The Breakfast of Spirit-Keepers

You can't learn without feedback, but not all feedback is helpful. Some is harmful. So—you guessed it—flow past this sort of feedback and don't let it hold you back.

Taking feedback is crucial for professional growth and business success. It's one of the factors often considered when people go through performance reviews. Being able to respond to feedback is important.

But not all feedback is created equal, and not all feedback is constructive. Some feedback, even from well-intentioned managers, can be biased, contradictory, or just plain wrong. This harmful feedback can be an obstacle in your path if you let it. Giving feedback is an essential management skill that all managers should be educated on. I have personally gone through outstanding management training on how to give constructive feedback. Some managers learn this skill sooner than others.

One of my mentees was once told his style was not a good cultural fit for the organization. This feedback wasn't constructive or work related. It was personal. And because he was not water, it stopped him in his tracks.

The tension here is that we both need to be open to accepting feedback to grow, but we also need to discern and recognize when feedback is not constructive and not let it hold us back. So how do you handle feedback that is not constructive or harmful? First, recognize it for what it is. Feedback that is personal, biased, contradictory, or not related to your actual work performance is likely not constructive. Second, don't internalize it. Flow past it like water around a rock. Take the useful and constructive feedback and leave the rest. And third, keep moving forward. Don't let poorly given feedback stop your progress.

Of course, as discussed in chapter 4, "Keeping Your (Metaphorical) Bags Packed," there are times when harmful feedback transforms from annoying to something that you should actively push back against. Knowing when to fight and when to flow is a skill that takes time, effort, and experience to master. If you let truly egregious feedback stand without a fight, you also risk losing your spirit.

Remember, the line between which feedback to flow around and which feedback to fight against can be thin and may vary depending on the severity, frequency, and context of the feedback. Trust your instincts, document patterns, and seek support from allies and mentors. If you have a good relationship with your HR partner, they can also be a good sounding board.

It's important to remember that when it comes to preserving your spirit, you're playing the long game. Not fighting every fight doesn't mean that you're not making a difference. As you flow around minor obstacles, you are gathering strength and support. Think of it like a river gathering water from tributaries. Each time you navigate around a boulder, you're not just avoiding the obstacle, but you're also forging a new path that others can follow. As your river grows stronger and wider, it will become more powerful, with the potential to wear down even the most stubborn of boulders. As more and more people follow your lead, the corporate culture itself will begin to shift. Eventually, you create a whole new streambed that supports your energy and keeps others' energy flowing forward as well.

Trust your instincts, gather your strength, and keep moving forward.

Underresourcing: A Dam in Your River

Resource constraints are a huge mass of boulders that can stop even the most determined water. At every company I've been with, underresourcing is a constant challenge.

Underresourcing burns people out, and many people find it hard to speak up about an effort being underresourced because they feel they should be carrying the load even when it is humanly impossible to do so.

So how do you handle this dam in your river?

1. **Clearly make the business case.** Document the impact the lack of resources is having on the business and what improvements would result from adequate resourcing.
2. **Make this business case early and often.** Bring other teams and organizations to amplify the need for additional resources.
3. **Communicate every lost sale or lost customer opportunity.** Highlight the consequences of not having proper resources in place by demonstrating the tangible losses to the business.

It's not easy, yet it is the only way to keep your river moving, to keep your spirit intact.

ROADBLOCK:

Not flowing around obstacles that aren't worth the energy to fight

CORE LESSONS CHAPTER NINE: BEING WATER

1. **Embrace adaptability.**

   Like water, learn to flow around obstacles and find alternative paths to reach your goals.

2. **Don't take it personally.**

   Recognize that many challenges in the corporate world are not personal but rather opportunities to practice resilience and find new ways forward.

3. **Keep moving.**

   Don't let setbacks or rejections stop you. Maintain your momentum and keep working toward your objectives.

4. **Be persistent.**

   Like water wearing down rock over time, be persistent in your efforts to navigate around obstacles and create change.

5. **Choose your battles.**

   Know when to flow around a challenge and when to stand your ground and fight for what's right.

6. **Ask yourself the following questions:**

- How might adopting a "be water" mindset change your career planning and development approach?
- How can you ensure that your pursuit of growth aligns with contributing to your team and company's success rather than becoming a "boulder" yourself?
- Can you think of some boulders you've known? How did you deal with them? Can you now see another way?

- Have you ever encountered a firm no in your career? Did you accept it? If so, how might you do things differently next time?

CONCLUSION

When I first started working on this book decades ago, I took a business trip to Singapore. During a few free hours, I decided to visit the shops of Orchard Street, which I had heard so much about from fellow business travelers. It was a popular tourist destination and also a great escape for weary business travelers. The vibrant energy of the streets, for me at least, boosted my spirit considerably. The humidity, on the other hand, took some getting used to.

I stepped into a shop packed with beautiful unique Asian souvenirs and collectibles. There were Buddha sculptures, carved jade dragons, and stunning silk clothes. I purchased a very special, small one-hundred-year-old wooden Buddha while I was there. I found the proprietor was watching a television program on a small TV behind the counter about Tibetan monks who lived in the mountains.

After perusing the wares, I went to the counter, and we both watched a segment about how it took the monks an entire week to get water back to the group on foot. I commented on the life they chose and the difficulties they faced. He told me that he was Buddhist and explained that the monks had refined the art of creating a rich inner life, one which gave them spiritual refuge that replenished their energy for their hard work.

He remarked to me that he had noticed a recent increase in Americans who passed through his shop articulating a commitment to spirituality. This was very strange to him. In his view "American" and "spirit" were opposites.

To help me understand what he meant by this, he told me about his encounter with a spiritual guru who came to his shop from India.

The guru walked straight in and said to the shopkeeper, "Ask me anything you want to know about your life."

The proprietor expressed his skepticism, letting him know that he didn't believe in that sort of thing and asking to know what he really wanted. The guru said, "Write anything you want on a piece of paper. While you do so, I'll go outside the shop and write the exact same thing."

The proprietor wrote his name in Chinese on a piece of paper, and indeed, the guru had written the same thing.

The proprietor, feeling both chagrined and inspired, told the guru that he was content with his life but asked if there was anything he should know about the future. The guru told him that he would have a child. Again, the proprietor was skeptical. His wife was forty-one, and the couple already had two grown children. But two years later, he became a father for the third time. Finally, he believed he had met a true guru, wise and in tune with his spirituality.

He took the time to explain this powerful story to me because he wanted me to understand the type of person he saw as connected to their spirituality. He said, "Including this guru, I have met only a few deeply wise and empathetic people—seers. But they all had one key thing in common: they had no possessions. This left their minds completely clear and free from material concerns."

I reflected on his words. I knew in my soul that the core of what he was saying had a deep truth to it. The world I was living in, in many ways, was devoid of spiritual purity. I understood his confusion at the idea of an American even trying to be in touch with their spirit. I told him, "I've also known only a small handful of people who kept their spirits intact and alive. However, they weren't gurus but everyday Americans with mortgages, car payments, emails, and a work-life integration at the center of the corporate world."

Understandably, he did not believe this was possible. He said, "Any person in a corporation inherently loses their spirit due to the environment." He noted the innate competitiveness and the implicit need to win at all costs in the game of the workplace.

This understanding of the corporate culture resonated with me, yet I knew deep down that Spirit-Keeping isn't a black-or-white game. Our world isn't divided into possession-less gurus and the spiritually dead. Though rare, I saw around me those who transcended the taxing demands of their workplace through the methods I've described in this book.

I wrote this book with the confidence of knowing that nurturing your spirit and seeking a life of meaning and purpose are pursuits each of us can undertake within the corporation. I can't explain how the guru and the shopkeeper wrote the same words on their pieces of paper. But I can explain how I and many like me live lives of reflection, intuition, and creativity within the bounds of our daily corporate lives.

We have competed at the highest levels, but we haven't lost ourselves in the process. The day we signed our employment contracts was not the day we checked our spirits at the door. We have mastered the delicate balance of observing the corporate rules without compromising our values. We have found the courage to live with integrity by listening to the voice of truth within.

I understand why the shopkeeper was dubious. I understand how many feel that the corporation is not a place for Spirit-Keepers. Or even if it is for a select few, that the struggle is not worth the effort and sacrifice. Yet I'm reminded as I close these pages of this book of where I started—in the hospital with my loved one.

I am so grateful that so many people were able to master both the material and spiritual worlds to create the enormous advances that kept him alive. Every piece of work, no matter how mundane it may seem, contributes to progress. The dedication and passion behind each task, combined with the desire to create something meaningful, ultimately propel us forward. The key is to find meaning and purpose in what we do, recognizing that every action, no matter how small, can contribute to our overall spiritual development. This perspective transforms work from a mere obligation into a meaningful pursuit that nurtures our spirits.

I hope that this book inspired you to fight the good fight. The work you do is important. The work corporations do is important. We are, in a metaphorical sense, toiling to carry water up our mountaintops, but what we bring to the top doesn't sustain just us—it sustains the world.

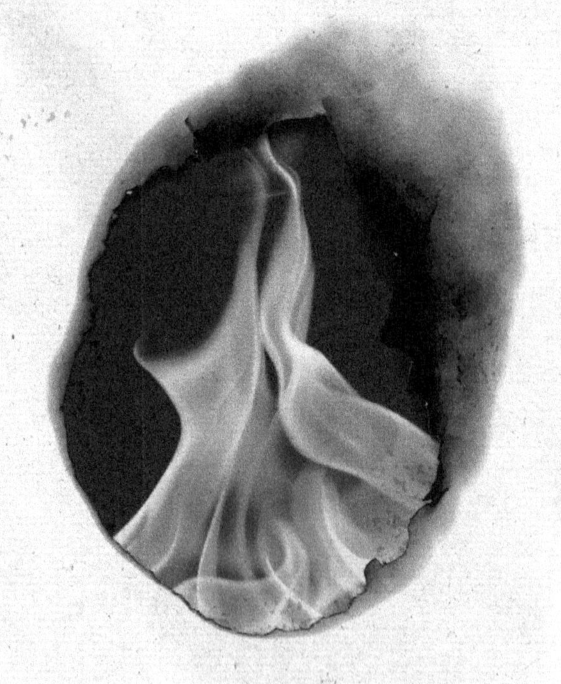

WHO AM I?

I am a corporate traveler, having grown up in the corporation for forty years, specifically in tech. I am a computer scientist who started in the advanced R & D lab working on cutting-edge local area network protocols and participated in one way or another in every major innovation and breakthrough along the way—through cloud and now generative AI. I am a Forbes AI contributor. I have dedicated myself to doing what I can to help pave the way for women in tech so they stay in tech.

I am a wife and mother who has always pushed the envelope in my work and life and has struggled to find and make time for my health. I believe I worked right on the edge of burnout, which is why I desperately wanted to write this book: to learn the lessons myself and because I know others struggle with this.

I have dedicated myself to trying to capture and document all I could in this book so you don't have to struggle. Maybe there is just one thing in here that will keep your inner fire burning. If that is the case, then this book is worth sharing with the world.